nigel marns

words
Nigel Marns

editor
Penny Marns

design and direction
Rosanna Marns

photography
Penny Marns and Roger Hamlin

copyright

printing
Printed by Booths Print, The Praze, Penryn, Cornwall, TR10 8AA, UK
ISBN 978-0-9566509-3-1
First Edition published by Saysomething Artbooks in Great Britain in 2017, 2nd edition 2019.

www.cornishcelticway.co.uk

pilgrims are persons
in motion passing
through territories
that are not
their own, seeking
something we might
call 'contemplation'
or perhaps the
word 'clarity' would
do as well, a goal to
which the spirit's
compass points the
way.

brother pedro of taizé,
quoted by ian bradley, pilgrimage: a
spiritual and cultural journey, 2009

co
en

45

there's something in the soil!

The Saints Way
St. Blazey to Luxulyan
Luxulyan to Helman Tor Gate
Eden Project Stop Off

55

being alive to the signs

The Saints Way
Helman Tor Gate to Lanivet
Lanivet to Withiel

63

companions on the way

The Saints Way
Withiel to St. Breock Downs
St. Breok Downs to St. Issey
St. Issey to Padstow

75

treasured finds

Padstow to Constantine Bay

83

refuge

Constantine Bay to St. Eval
St. Eval to St. Mawgan

91

land, air and water

St. Mawgan to Watergate Bay
Watergate Bay to Newquay

99

secrets uncovered

Newquay to Crantock
Crantock to Holywell
Holywell to St. Piran's Oratory

111

good samaritans

St. Piran's Oratory to St. Agnes
St. Agnes to Porthtowan

Route map

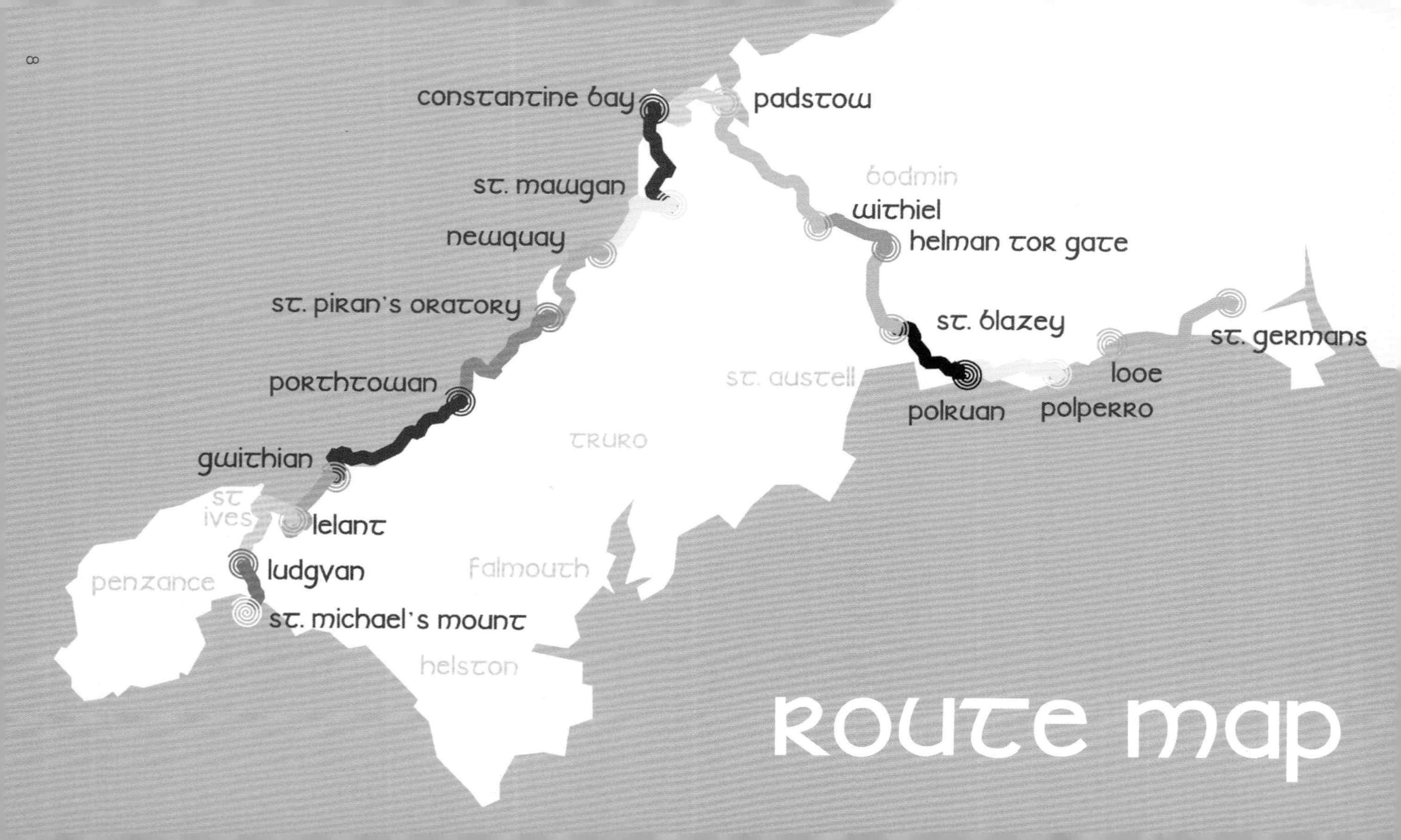

constantine bay
padstow
st. mawgan
bodmin
withiel
newquay
helman tor gate
st. piran's oratory
st. blazey
st. germans
st. austell
looe
porthtowan
polruan
polperro
truro
gwithian
st ives
lelant
ludgvan
falmouth
penzance
st. michael's mount
helston

It is not known to what extent Cornwall was Christianised by the time the Romans left Britain in 410, how strong was the influence of the Roman Empire, or how many of the Cornish folk had met early Christians in their seafaring and trading activities. However, it is certain that Christianity was brought to Cornwall between the fifth and seventh century by many men and women from Ireland and Wales and that their impact on Cornwall was huge. Ninety of these Celtic saints are encountered along this Cornish Celtic Way.

I have a passionate interest in these Cornish Celtic saints. They left behind crosses, chapels and holy wells; their names remain in many hundreds of villages and places in Cornwall. They left their inspirational stories too. To connect to them and their extraordinary lives, we have to walk in their footsteps.

This book is a combination of different genres. It is a guidebook with maps and directions for each section of this Cornish Celtic Way through Cornwall from St. Germans to St. Michael's Mount. It contains some history of the Celtic saints and includes poems, songs and reflections inspired by encounters with them in each place, giving an introduction to Celtic spirituality. For those seeking a spiritual quest or a retreat this book could be used as a handbook, for a living, breathing, spiritual experience and asks the question: how can encounters with the Cornish Celtic saints enhance our spirituality today? Finally, this book is a journal of a walk undertaken in April 2016, and I have included my own observations to encourage other walkers to observe and find encounters along the way. I also reflect on the Eden Project, a special place that has emerged in recent times, and on the questing nature of surfing.

This suggested pilgrimage route from St. Germans to St. Michael's Mount through Cornwall is not definitive. I hope it will inspire others and lead to the exploration of further routes and connections in the future. There are still immense Celtic treasures to be found...

how to use this book

A Cornish Celtic Way is divided into 16 themed chapters. Each chapter contains the following sections detailed below. These are provided as a set of tools to help as you set about your walk and pilgrimage. Use these in a way that works for you: choose to use all of the sections, or just focus on a few.

maps and directions

These are your practical tools to navigate the route. For each map there is an estimated time and mileage, based on an average walking pace of 2.7 miles per hour. The scale of the maps are shown by the 1km blue grid sqaures, and each walk has been given a grading of easy, moderate or challenging. You may choose to supplement the book maps with OS maps.

information on saints and places

These sections tell the story of places along the route - the history of the Cornish Celtic saints and their influence and heritage in the landscape.

action

These are to encourage you to have a physical interaction with things you may experience along the route.

questions

The questions are to prompt thoughts and reflections as you walk.

christian references

These extracts from Christian texts and the Bible relate to the theme of the chapter, and provide a focus and Christian grounding to inspire you on your pilgrimage. Further information on 'walking as pilgrimage' is found in Chapter 17.

personal reflection

These are comments from the author's experiences when walking the route.

map key

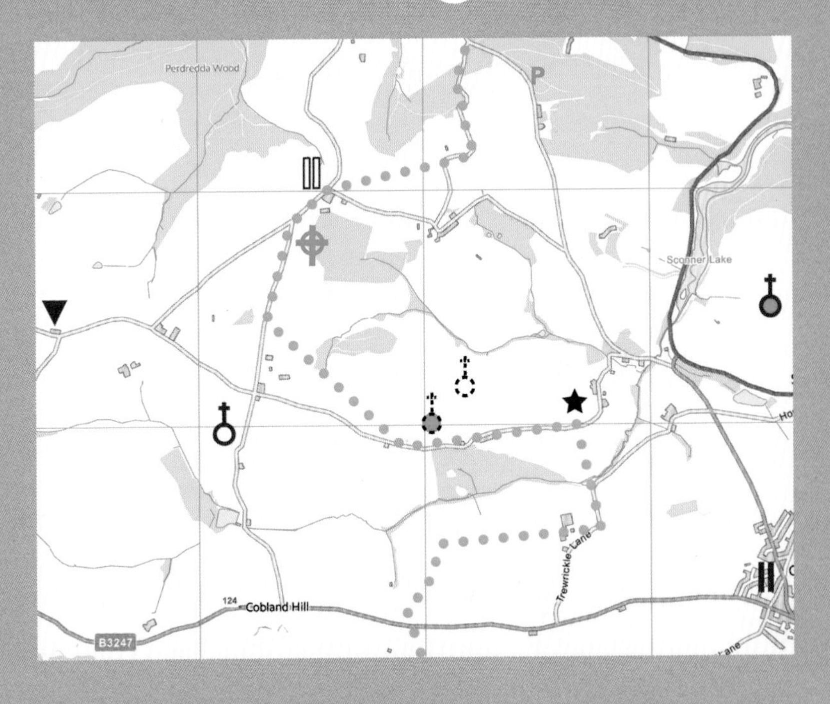

route

church or chapel

church or chapel with celtic cross

celtic cross

facilities

car park

ruins

ruins with celtic cross

place of interest

minimal facilities

hostel

"Piping down the valleys wild,
Piping songs of pleasant glee,
On a cloud I saw a child,
And he laughing said to me:

"Pipe a song about a lamb"
So I piped with merry cheer.
"Piper, pipe that song again".
So he wept with joy to hear.

"Drop thy pipe, thy happy pipe,
Sing thy songs of happy cheer"
So I sang the same again,
While he wept with joy to hear.

"Piper, sit thee down and write
In all a book that all may read"
So he vanished from my sight;
And I plucked a hollow reed,

And I made a rural pen,
And I stained the water clear,
And I wrote my happy songs,
Every child may joy to hear"

William Blake, Introduction to Songs of Innocence, 1789

chapter 1

doorways, portals and pathways

st. germans - seaton - looe

DISTANCE: 5.5MILES/9KM | TIME: 2HOURS | DIFFICULTY: EASY

St. Germans to Seaton

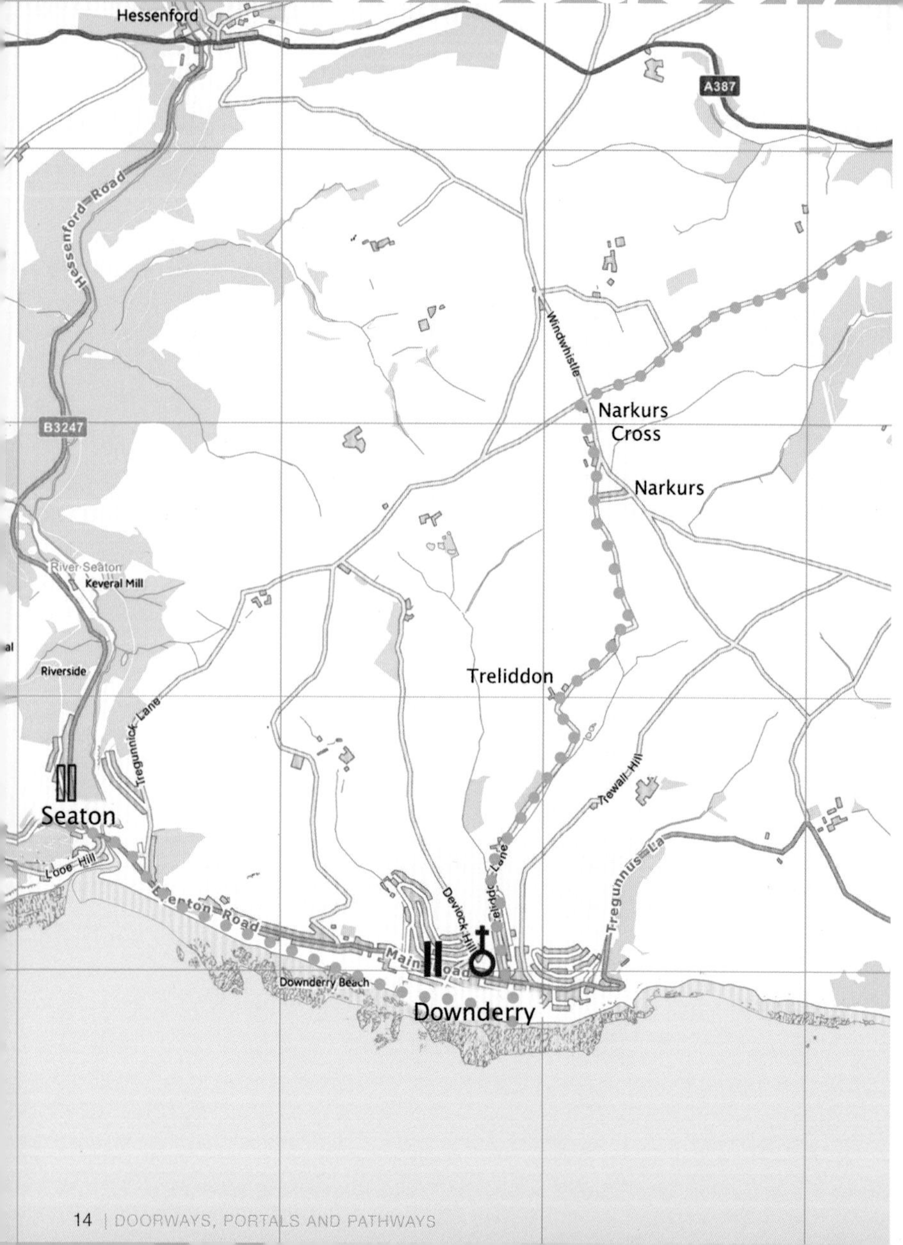

Hessenford
A387
Hessenford Road
Windwhistle
Narkurs Cross
Narkurs
B3247
River Seaton
Keveral Mill
Riverside
Treliddon
Tregunnick Lane
Trewall Hill
Seaton
Looe Hill
Tregunnus La
Deviock Hill
Eglarooze Lane
Main Road
Downderry Beach
Downderry

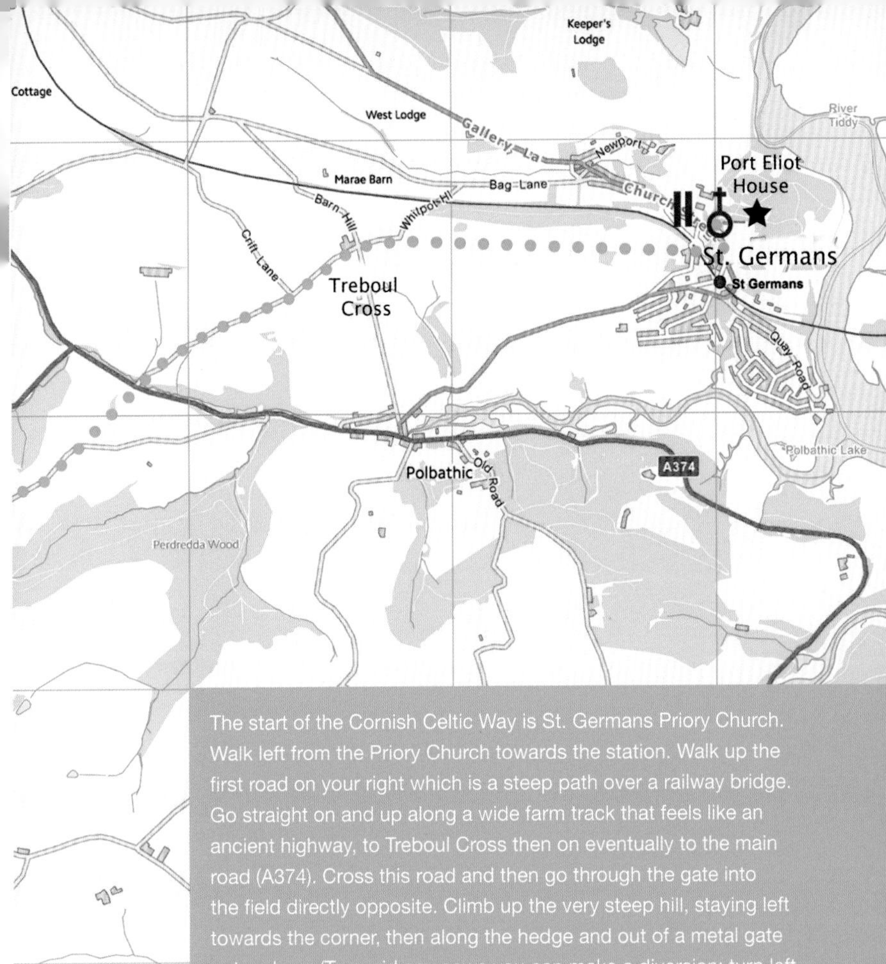

The start of the Cornish Celtic Way is St. Germans Priory Church. Walk left from the Priory Church towards the station. Walk up the first road on your right which is a steep path over a railway bridge. Go straight on and up along a wide farm track that feels like an ancient highway, to Treboul Cross then on eventually to the main road (A374). Cross this road and then go through the gate into the field directly opposite. Climb up the very steep hill, staying left towards the corner, then along the hedge and out of a metal gate onto a lane. (To avoid any cows you can make a diversion: turn left at the A374, then take a right onto the lane). Follow this gently-inclining high-hedged lane for half an hour to Narkus Cross, turn left at the cross-roads into the village of Narkus, going through the village and past the phone box and 'Natural Salad Growers'. Take the right hand signpost to Treliddon that leads to Downderry. Just before Treliddon you get a glimpse of the sea. You drop down slightly emerging at Downderry Primary School and St. Nicolas Church and Chapel. Take the footpath alongside the school down to the beach. You can walk to Seaton along the beach and/or the sea wall providing the tide is not too high. At high tide you can leave the beach part way along or alternatively walk all the way on the road parallel to the beach.

St. Germans

action

As you first approach the church at St. Germans, you will immediately see a number of stone doorways, porches and portals. Doorways and portals can be physical and spiritual gateways to new experiences and perhaps, as writer Philip Sheldrake says, 'transit points' to other worlds. As you pass through the ancient porch-way and step into the grandeur of the church at St. Germans, you are daring to cross such a threshold. Be open to the experiences and encounters that you have here and along the Cornish Celtic Way.

Go outside to the west door - a highly decorated, carved stonework Norman doorway, dating from c1185 which John Spence, a former vicar at St. Germans, described as 'the noblest portal in Cornwall'. The central inscription reads 'INHR' which stands in Latin for 'in his service'. Before you set off, touch the centre-piece of this door - it could feel like pressing a start button; a physical action to help propel you forward.

questions

Why are you going on pilgrimage? Do you feel ready for it? Is it to have a good walk, a rest, or to see some beautiful countryside? Maybe you won't know yet; the reason will arise as you think, pray and meditate and have experiences along the way. How much of your journey will be new and exciting? Do you feel that you will be returning to your roots?

Are you seeking to find renewal and refreshment and new revelations, doorways, portals and possibilities?

christian references

God said to Abraham: 'Go from your country, your people and your father's household to the land I will show you. I will make you into a great nation, and I will bless you; I will make your name great, and you will be a blessing. I will bless those who bless you... and all peoples on earth will be blessed through you.' *(Genesis 12: 1-3)*

By faith Abraham.. obeyed and went even though he did not know where he was going. *(Hebrews 11:8)*

st. germanus

St. Germanus *(380-448)* was a French saint and the Bishop of Auxerre who taught St. Illtud and St. Patrick *(385-461)* and it was St. Patrick who later made St. Germanus a bishop. It is believed that St. Germanus personally established the monastery named after him at St. Germans as early as 428, making it one of the earliest church sites in Cornwall and Britain. St. Germanus is associated with Rame parish in south east Cornwall, and a chapel near Padstow is also dedicated to him, as well as many churches in Brittany. However, St. Germanus is a controversial figure: he was sent to Britain to argue against the British 'heretic' Pelagius, who is credited with inspiring many Celtic Christian ideas. St. Germanus' relics may have been laid to rest at St. Germans in the Medieval period. Near the site of this Priory Church, on the Port Eliot estate, there was an enclosed and fortified Celtic village of which no ruins remain.

st. conan

Up until 926, the Christian church in Cornwall had followed a Celtic monastic model. Then King Athelstan set up a Cornish diocese on Saxon lines and St. Germans became the seat of the first Cornish bishop, Conan (not 'Conan the Barbarian' of Arnold Schwarzenegger's first film!). Conan, though a Cornish Christian, was appointed as abbot-bishop at St. Germans in order to help bring the Celtic church into line with Roman ways and practices. For a while, St. Germans was the cathedral church of Cornwall and there were five successive Saxon bishops until 1050 when Cornwall came under the jurisdiction of the Bishop of Exeter. It was not then until 1877 that a separate diocese and bishop was again established to serve Cornwall exclusively. A Victorian chapel in Egloshayle parish (Washaway) was dedicated to St. Conan.

st. winwaloe

St. Winwaloe was one of the most famous saints of Brittany. He trained under the Irish St. Budoc in Brittany and founded an abbey at Landevénnec. Several shrines in Cornwall are dedicated to him: Landewednack, Gunwalloe on the Lizard Peninsula, and at Towednack in West Penwith; also a hamlet close to St. Germans bears his name (St. Winnols). St. Winwaloe is credited for never sitting

downderry beach

down in church and was a vegetarian and healer. He healed a childhood friend's leg damaged in a game and retrieved his sister's eye that had been pecked out by a goose: he identified the offending goose from the flock, cut it open and restored the eye to the socket! St. Winwaloe may have been from a Cornish or Welsh family who had moved to Brittany before he was born. (Winwaloe's sister, Chreibia, had a Welsh name.)

action

As you walk along the beach towards Seaton, you will see many striking pink rocks. There are also many pebbles on this beach with white lines across them suggesting pathways. Choose one to mark the beginning of your journey.

personal reflection

The pebble I chose seemed to show lots of paths. I wondered if I would often go wrong in search of the destination. Some pathways could be dead ends, some lead me forward.

questions

Are you on this pilgrimage because you are seeking a new path for your life? Has your life, as mine had, come to a cul de sac or dead end? Carry your pathway pebble with you on your pilgrimage. Have you found it difficult to get on the road? Do you find the ways 'narrow' or the path before you 'expansive and wide open'? Have you made false turns, taken wrong or strange pathways in your life? Is there a 'true' path for everyone to follow or do we have to find our own paths through individual choice?

Round the corners of the world I turn, More and more about the world I learn; And the new things that I see, You'll be looking at along with me: And it's from the old I travel to the new; Keep me travelling along with you.

Sydney Carter, One More Step, 1915-2004

DISTANCE: 3.5MILES/5.5KM | TIME: 1.5HOURS | DIFFICULTY: MODERATE

seaton to looe

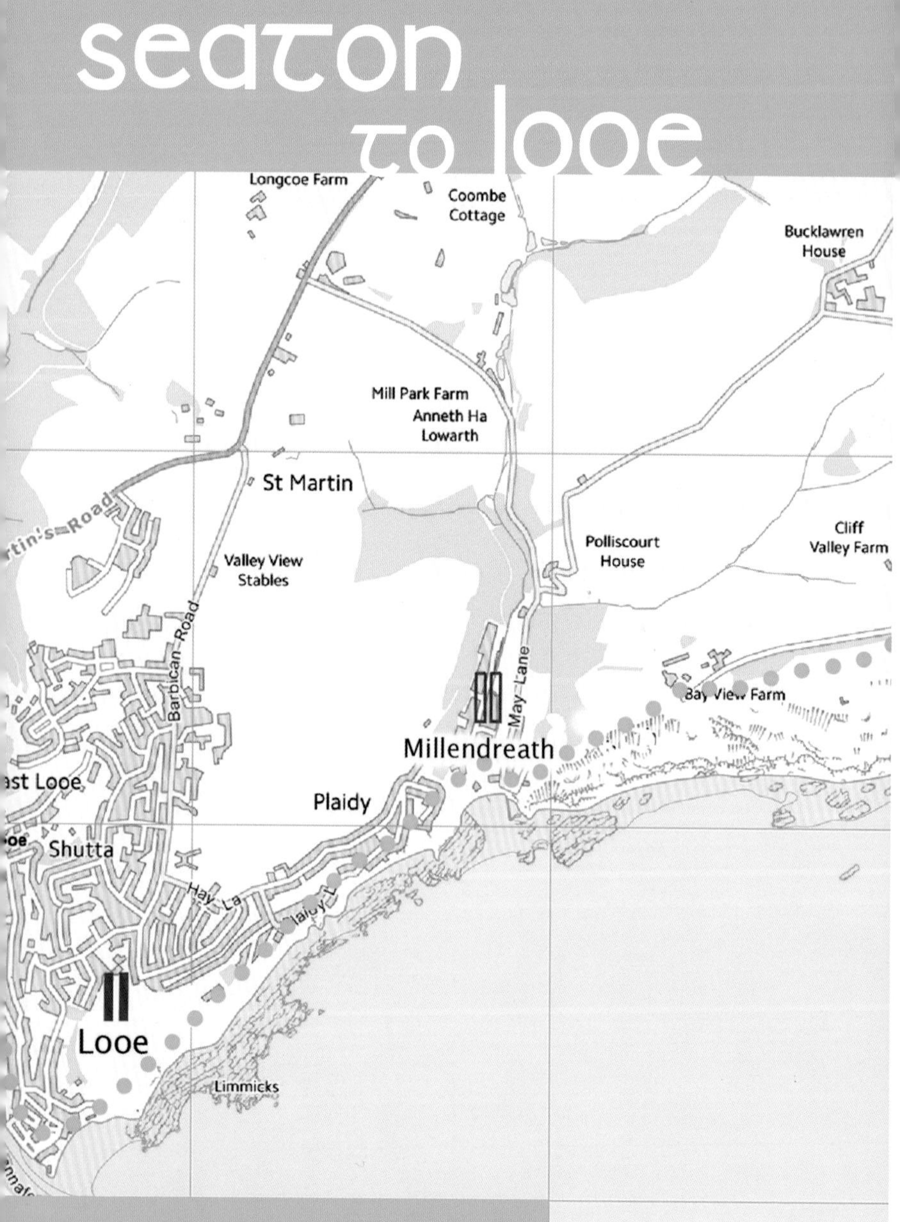

From Seaton, walk along the coast path to Looe. It is steep and difficult in places. The coast path is now diverted onto a stretch of road due to coastal erosion near the Monkey Sanctuary.

notes on this walk:

personal reflection

You will pass many grand 1980s-built holiday homes with Greek- inspired curly metal balconies, white walls and port-holes. You will also see more modern holiday homes and the 1970s resort built into the hillside of Black Rock at Millendreath. All these properties made me think of different people's aspirations and idyllic places.

questions

What are your dreams and aspirations? Do you have a destination towards which you are travelling? Where do you want to end up or escape to? Do you have a picture of heaven or paradise that you carry with you as you journey on through life?

love all of god's creation, the whole of it and every grain of sand in it. love every leaf, every ray of god's light, love the animals, love the plants, love everything. if you love everything you will perceive the divine mystery in all things and learn to comprehend it better every day.

f. dostoevsky, the brothers karamazov, 1880

chapter 2

lonely places and comforting creatures

looe - polperro

DISTANCE: 4.5MILES/7KM | TIME: 2.5HOURS | DIFFICULTY: MODERATE

looe to polperro

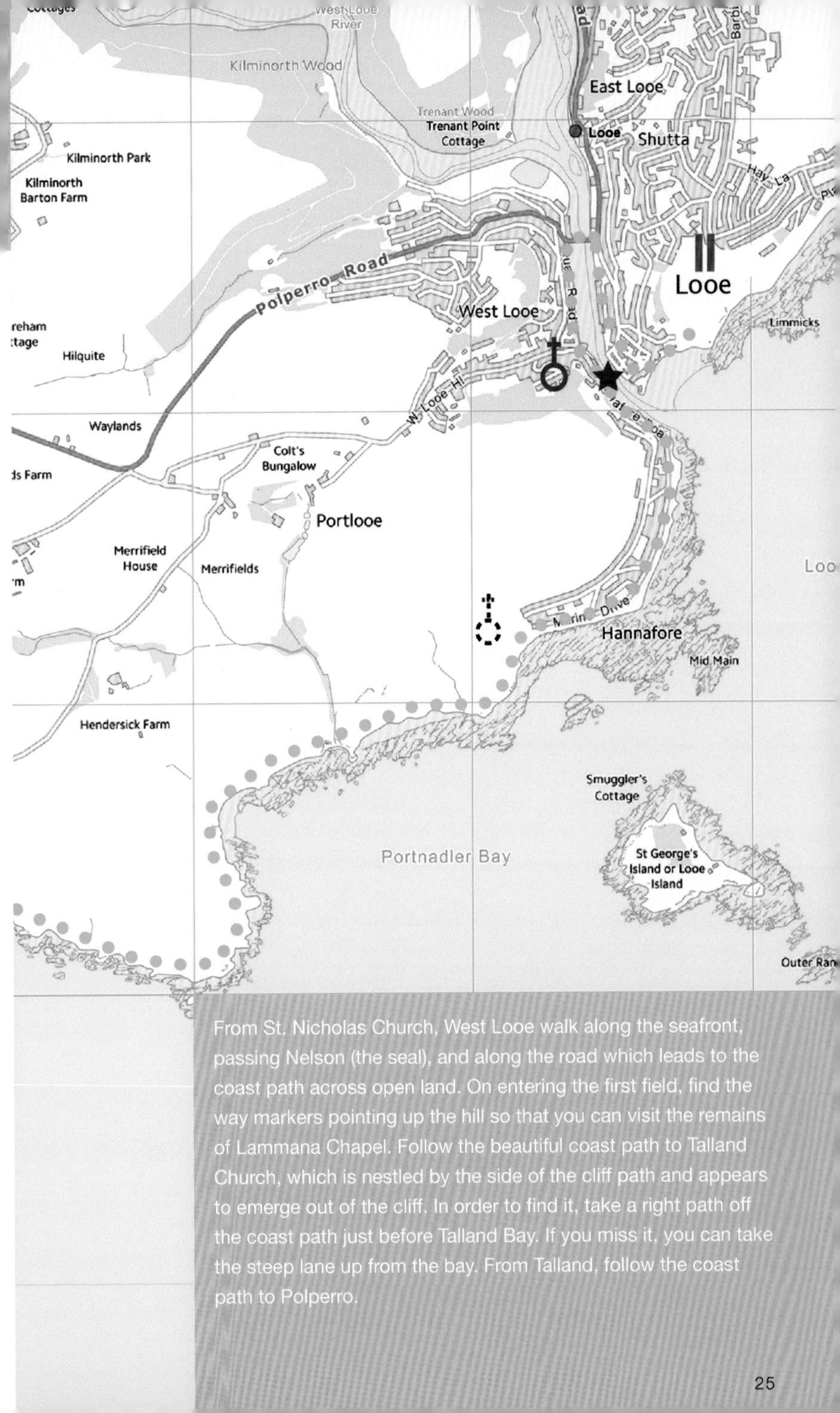

From St. Nicholas Church, West Looe walk along the seafront, passing Nelson (the seal), and along the road which leads to the coast path across open land. On entering the first field, find the way markers pointing up the hill so that you can visit the remains of Lammana Chapel. Follow the beautiful coast path to Talland Church, which is nestled by the side of the cliff path and appears to emerge out of the cliff. In order to find it, take a right path off the coast path just before Talland Bay. If you miss it, you can take the steep lane up from the bay. From Talland, follow the coast path to Polperro.

st. nicholas church

This church was used as an almshouse and a guildhall in the thirteenth century. As well as being Father Christmas, St Nicholas is also the patron saint of sailors - an appropriate saint for a church situated on the quayside.

personal reflection

A seal named Nelson lived in Looe harbour for twenty five years and is honoured by the quayside sculpture. Nelson reminded me of stories of St. Cuthbert *(634-687)*, the Northumbrian Celtic saint who had his feet dried by friendly seals (as recorded by the historian Bede). The Celtic saints worked with nature and formed close bonds with other creatures. Animals can be our companions too: when I visited Lammana chapel a robin was singing.

action

As you journey on be aware of the animals and birds who are accompanying and encouraging you.

lammana chapel

Lammana Chapel is the first of many Celtic chapels on the Cornish Celtic Way. Celtic Christians were drawn to the edges: often they chose remote spots close to the coast to set up their cells, perhaps with the opportunity to look out over the seas towards their homelands, or more because they were influenced by the example of the Egyptian and Syrian Desert Fathers, a movement seeking spiritual purity and started by St. Anthony in late 300. Philip Sheldrake says that Celtic Christians regarded edges as 'boundary places' between the material and spiritual worlds, 'thin places where the membrane is permeable'. The historian, Finney, evidencing Egyptian and Syrian graves in Ireland, believed that this middle-Eastern desert tradition was brought to Ireland by the established trade routes and adapted by John Cassian and Martin of Tours. The historian, Hastings, claimed that 'Celtic monasticism was simply oriental mysticism replacing the desert with the rocky islands of the Atlantic seaboard'.

There is a legend that the cloth-trader, Joseph of Arimathea, brought Jesus to Cornwall and came to Lammana Chapel when Jesus was a boy. Some people in Cornwall believe that this is why the land is so blessed; because Jesus himself may have walked upon it. Indeed, William Blake's poem and hymn *'Jerusalem'* is inspired by this tale: 'And did those feet in ancient time, walk upon England's mountains green? And was the holy Lamb of God on England's pleasant pastures seen?'

personal reflection

I found Lammana chapel to be a strong and compelling site, as so much of the shape of the old chapel is still in evidence from so many centuries before: there is a small nave altar. Services are still celebrated here.

looe island

optional extra - looe island

If you are travelling in summer and the weather is good, you could catch the boat to Looe Island (which was once called Lammana Island or St. George's Island) to see the remains of the older sister chapel of Lammana. Fires were lit here to avoid shipwrecks. The Celtic saints were enchanted by habitable islands just off the mainland. The easternmost Isles of Scilly were inhabited entirely by monks and hermits, the historian, Doble, claimed. St. Columba founded his community on the remote Scottish island of Iona, and St. Cuthbert not only used the off-shore and tidal Lindisfarne Island in Northumbria, but withdrew even further to the Farne Islands for much of his ministry. These saints saw islands as strange, magical, 'other' places. There is a legend of giants living on Looe Island. Cornwall has several giants' legends - including that of the giant at St. Michael's Mount.

questions

What are the places of importance, the places of magic or encounter for you? Where are the places of meeting with God?

talland church

Talland Church suddenly appears behind the cliff path. This is the first of many ancient holy sites whose appearance on the skyline is a marker to encourage and lead onwards. Talland Church is the main church of the area. It has a separate tower and had a link to Launceston Priory and the Benedictine abbey at Glastonbury. In the Cornish language *'tal'* means *'brow of a hill'* and *'lan'* means *'holy place'* so that it is not believed that there was ever a saint named 'Tallan'. The present altar at Talland Church is on the site of a Celtic altar. Talland Church stands on a ley line and is close to a constant stream of water.

polperro

Polperro has many narrow streets and is a typical Cornish fishing village with a museum of fishing and smuggling.

personal reflection

The hill from Talland to Polperro is very steep. It made me reflect on people whose journeys are very hard and difficult. You might have come on the Cornish Celtic Way to get away from it all or leave the world and its problems behind you. However, it is important that these concerns are not completely forgotten. As I walked along this difficult path I thought and prayed about the refugees fleeing war to an uncertain and unknown future, often living in squalid borderland detention centres. Many people struggle in life and the struggle up a hill can echo this.

I met many companions along the way who blessed my journey. On the very first day I met someone that I recognised. Meeting him was a great blessing and I felt that God had placed him in my path. Then today there were four encouraging greetings: the bus driver, a man walking along the quay near the sculpture of Nelson the seal, a young woman walking her dog who warned me that the way to Polperro was steep, and at Polperro two Salvation Army captains who blessed my journey and my proposal for this Cornish Celtic Way.

chapter 3

unsung heroines and lights

polperro - lansallos - st. wyllow church - polruan

DISTANCE: 5.25MILES/8.5KM | TIME: 3.5HOURS | DIFFICULTY: MODERATE

polperro to St. Wyllow church

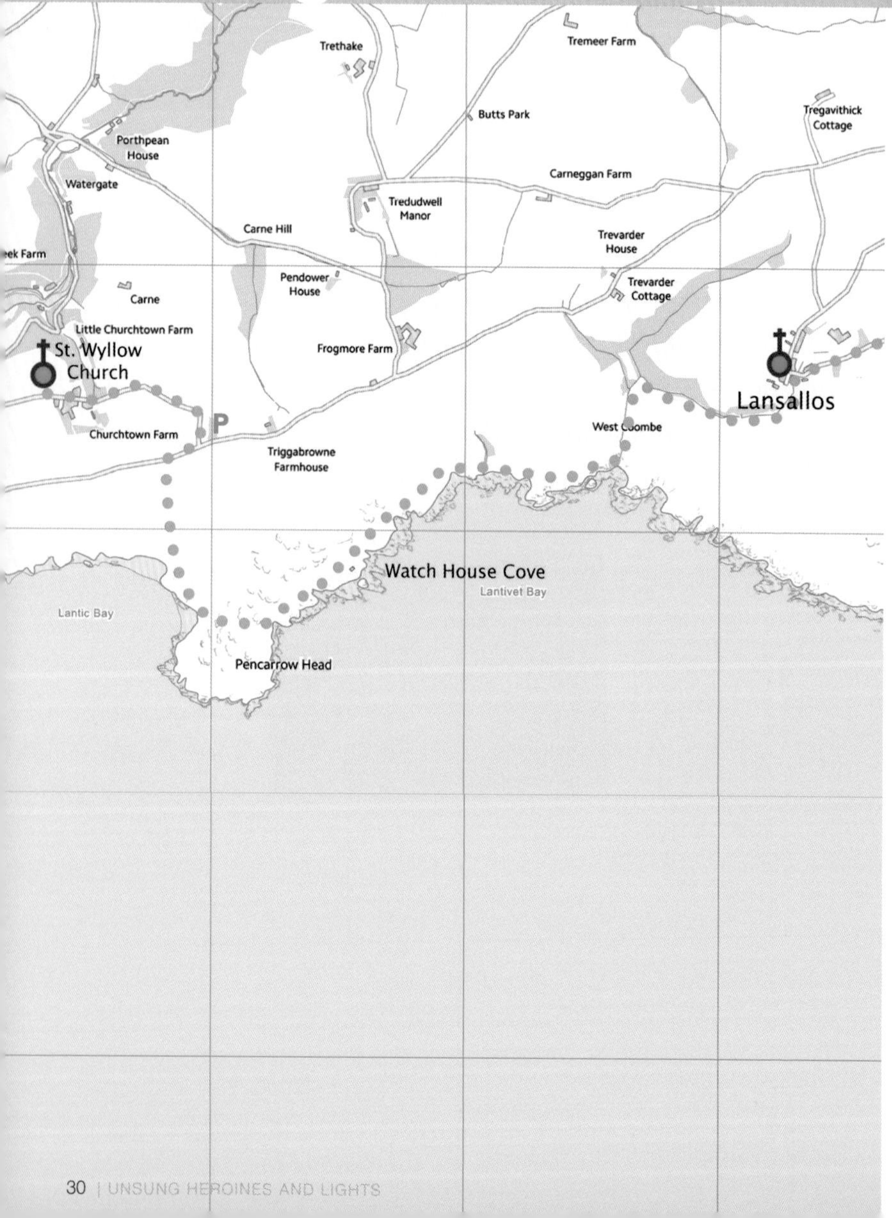

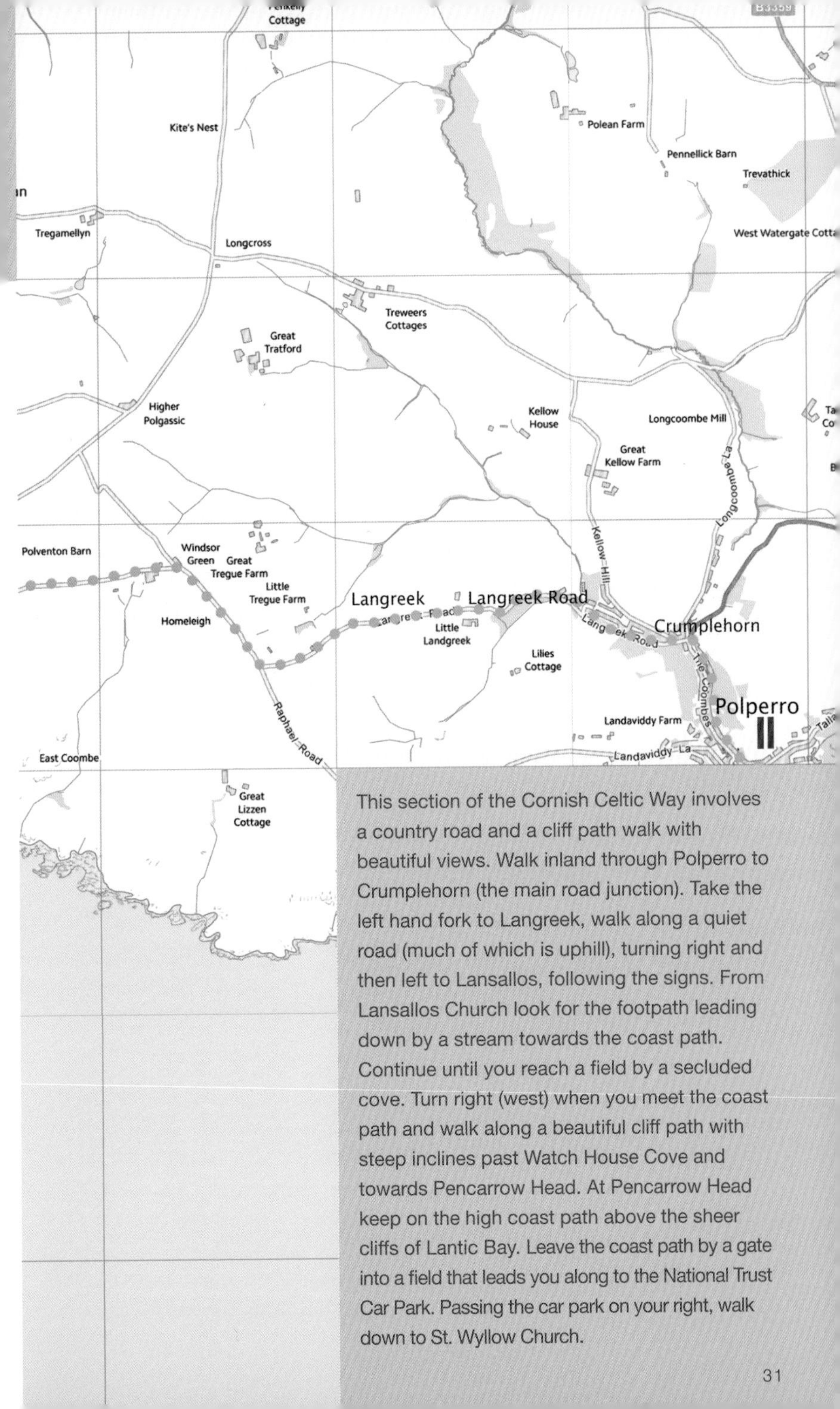

This section of the Cornish Celtic Way involves a country road and a cliff path walk with beautiful views. Walk inland through Polperro to Crumplehorn (the main road junction). Take the left hand fork to Langreek, walk along a quiet road (much of which is uphill), turning right and then left to Lansallos, following the signs. From Lansallos Church look for the footpath leading down by a stream towards the coast path. Continue until you reach a field by a secluded cove. Turn right (west) when you meet the coast path and walk along a beautiful cliff path with steep inclines past Watch House Cove and towards Pencarrow Head. At Pencarrow Head keep on the high coast path above the sheer cliffs of Lantic Bay. Leave the coast path by a gate into a field that leads you along to the National Trust Car Park. Passing the car park on your right, walk down to St. Wyllow Church.

lansallos

lansallos church

The church of St. Ildierna, Lansallos dominates the land around it as a way mark. *'Lan'* means *'holy place'* and *'Salwys'* means *'Saviour'*. In the churchyard there is a Celtic cross, and part of a Celtic font has been moved from there into the church by the altar. Much of the church is of fifteenth century origin.

st. ildierna

The early Celtic church had few divisions between men and women and it was considered quite normal that women should lead communities. Jesus demonstrated a radically inclusive approach to women and they formed a large part of Jesus' entourage. St. Hilda *(614-680)* led a community of both men and women, a 'double-monastery' at Whitby, and St. Bridget led a large monastery at Kildare in Ireland. However, many like St. Ildierna were less known. Some records show St. Ildierna to be a man but she has a feminine ending to her Latin name. In fact, a lot of Cornish churches are named after women. These women travelled from Wales and Ireland to bring Christianity to Cornwall.

christian reference

Jesus travelled about from one town and village to another, proclaiming the good news of the kingdom of God. The Twelve were with him, and also some women who had been cured of evil spirits and diseases: Mary (called Magdalene) from whom seven demons had come out; Joanna the wife of Chuza, the manager of Herod's household; Susanna; and many others. These women were helping to support them out of their own means. *(Luke 8:1-3).*

questions

In a world of social media self-promotion and keen celebrity interest, how important for you is it that your name and what you do is remembered and recorded? Who are our lights and guides? Who are the famous women or men or heroes and heroines in your day-to-day life? Are they known only to you, are they 'unsung heroines' or are they known to many?

action

Find the Celtic cross; only the upper portion remains in the churchyard to the west of the tower. This was found by a local farmer whilst ploughing the adjacent field. It was placed in the churchyard in the last century. The circular slot is thought to have supported a torch. As you touch this cross think about your 'lights and guides', and carry their influence, light and guidance as you travel onwards.

st. wyllow church

Travel writer, Diana Pé described this church as 'spacious, light, simple and sure' and it has a fourteenth century wagon roof. St.Wyllow Church is isolated and was built as a central point to serve Polruan and the four scattered hamlets of the peninsula and you can imagine worshippers walking along the lanes from all these places up to the church. The church is also a significant place for another woman: writer and novelist Daphne du Maurier who was married here in 1932. The church appears as Lanoc Church in her first novel *'The Loving Spirit'*.

The porch door frame has a carved eighth century *'XP'* (this is the Greek *'chi-ro'* for Christ). There is a thirteenth century stone lantern cross at the south porch. There are two more lantern crosses along the Cornish Celtic Way.

st. wyllow

The historian, Catherine John, relates that St.Wyllow was an Irishman who came to Fowey. On his arrival he was guided by helpful fish across the estuary and up Pont Pill, where he established a hermitage. St.Wyllow means *'the valley church'*; the original church was half a mile north from the present site at the head of the creek. St.Wyllow was beheaded by Melyn ys Kyrenrede and legend tells that he picked up his own head and carried it to the site where the present church is built.

question

St.Wyllow was killed for his faith. What do you hold most precious in your life? How important is this to you?

DISTANCE: 1.5MILES/2.5KM | TIME: 0.6HOURS | DIFFICULTY: EASY

St. Wyllow Church to Polruan

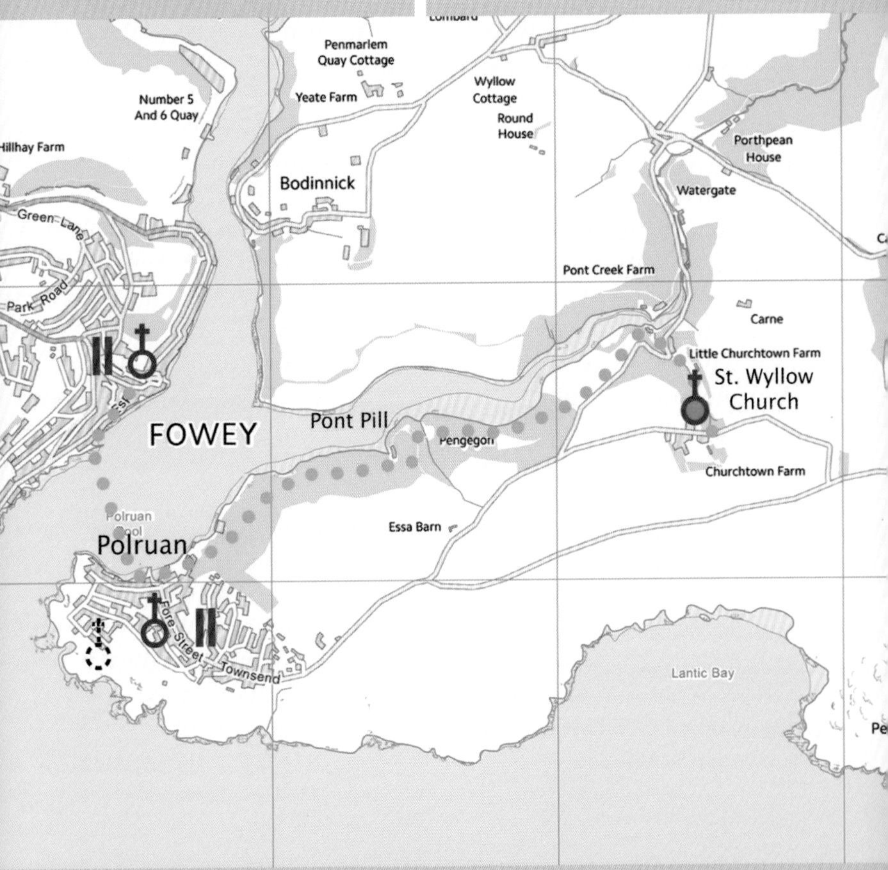

The National Trust has constructed a walk from St. Wyllow Church: on leaving the church main door walk left and follow the path out the back of the churchyard and down towards the creek of Pont Pill. Follow the signs to Polruan along the valley with the creek down below on your right. This takes you through woodland and along fields. The path is called 'Hall Walk'. Avoid a path forking right down to the shoreline. On arrival in Polruan you need to catch the foot ferry to Fowey, but first you can visit the headland across the town. Climb through the interesting streets of Polruan up to the headland where you can find the ruins of St. Saviour's Chapel and amazing views out to sea and of Readymoney Cove where the walk continues across the estuary.

christian reference

Jesus said: 'You are the light of the world. A town built on a hill cannot be hidden. Neither do people light a lamp and put it under a bowl. Instead they put it on its stand, and it gives light to everyone in the house. In the same way, let your light shine before others, that they may see your good deeds and glorify your Father in heaven'.
(Matthew 5:14-16)

St. Saviour's Celtic chapel, Polruan

After the lantern cross at Lanteglos Church, there is another point of light in Polruan on the headland: the remains of the ancient Celtic chapel of St. Saviour. The chapel was solidly built and the buttress is still standing. In Celtic times a monk lived here on St. Saviour's Hill, maintaining a light in order to steer ships to safety, preventing shipwreck and guiding them into the estuary harbour. The chapel was also used by the monks to spot the approach of enemy ships, becoming Polruan's first coastguard tower. The modern coastguard station appropriately sits alongside the ancient chapel.

At Polruan, the chapel was dedicated to 'The Saviour', Christ himself. Local historian, Frances Eileen Burdett, suggested that Jesus alone was considered to be strong enough to protect seafarers from disaster and shipwreck. In her story of St. Saviour's Church at Polruan, she notes that on some Celtic crosses there is a picture of a young boy. Could this indicate that Jesus did indeed come to Cornwall? Could this harbour be the place where Joseph of Arimathea first brought Jesus?

chapter 4

conflict and crossing

polruan - fowey - st. blazey

DISTANCE: 6MILES/9.5KM | TIME: 2.5HOURS | DIFFICULTY: EASY

polruan to st. blazey

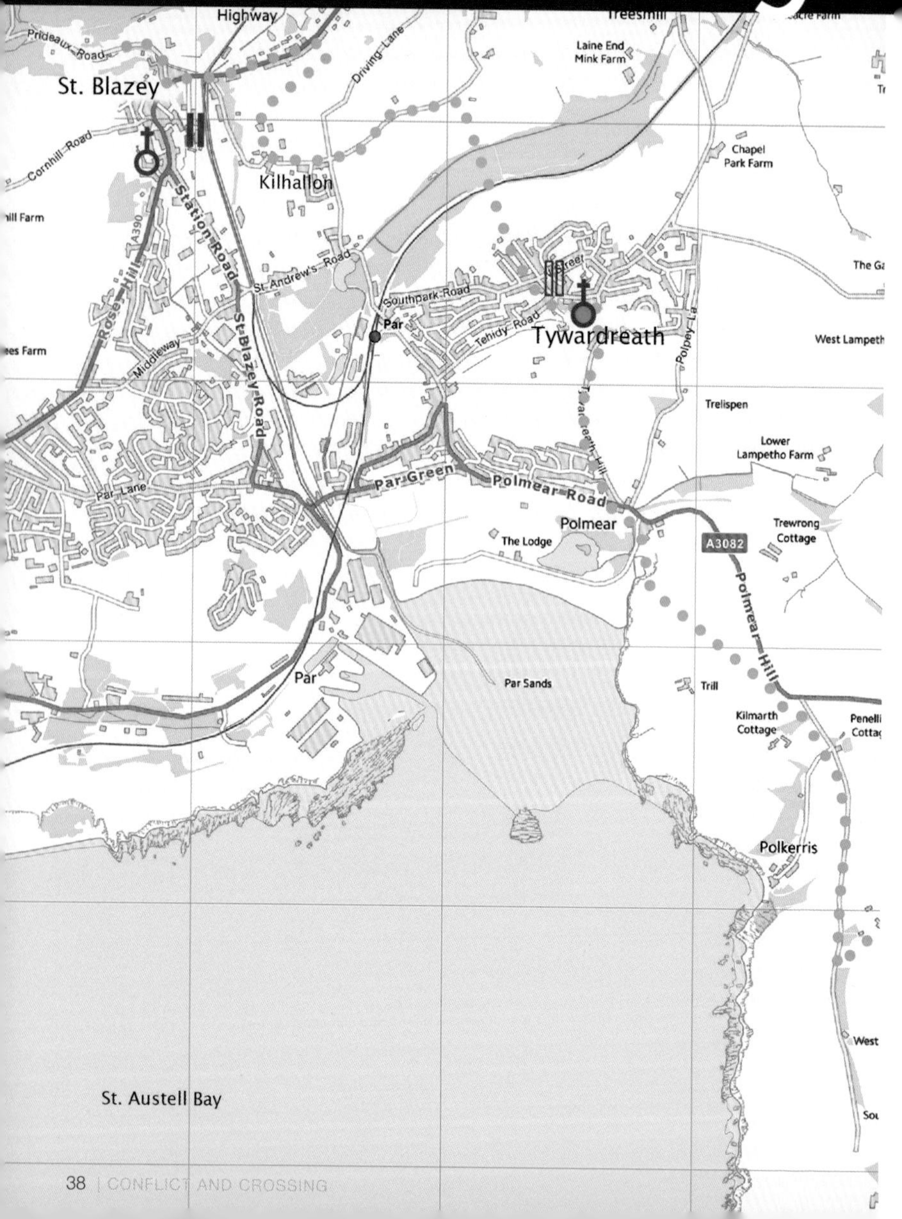

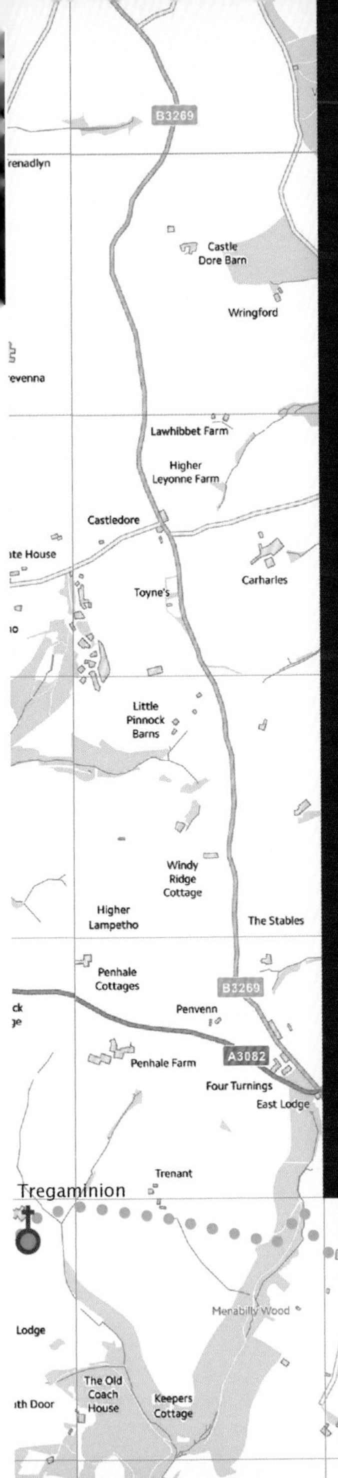

Cross the estuary by ferry to Fowey. There are clear 'Saints Way' signs all the way from Fowey to Padstow. You can supplement the maps and directions in this book with the excellent Saints Way guides. However, the Saints Way, rather confusingly, has two alternative routes between Fowey and Helman Tor Gate. This Cornish Celtic Way follows the route via St. Blazey that leaves the church at Fowey in a seaward direction- that is, walking out of Fowey with the estuary on your left. Follow the Saints Way signs to Readymoney Cove where the path turns inland through woodland, uphill. The path joins lanes to Lankelly Farm and then down a valley, across a stream and on up through woodland and open land and farms. Find Tregaminion Chapel which has Celtic crosses outside. Go onto the lane and turn right and then at the T-junction of the A3082 turn left. After a short distance, left again into fields overlooking St. Austell Bay. Cross the first field to the middle of the right hand boundary and then diagonally to the coast path leading down to the road at Polmear. Go under the old railway bridge and take the second right turning, which is the lane to Tywardreath, finding the church in Church Street. From the church, turn left, continuing down Church Street, ignoring Tehidy Road and straight over into Wood Lane at the junction. This lane leads into a valley, crosses the railway and reaches a road. Turn left and go across at the crossroads. In Kilhallon, turn right following the Saints Way path until you reach the main road (A390). Turn left towards St. Blazey and cross the railway again, noting where the Saints Way continues along Prideaux Road opposite the petrol station.

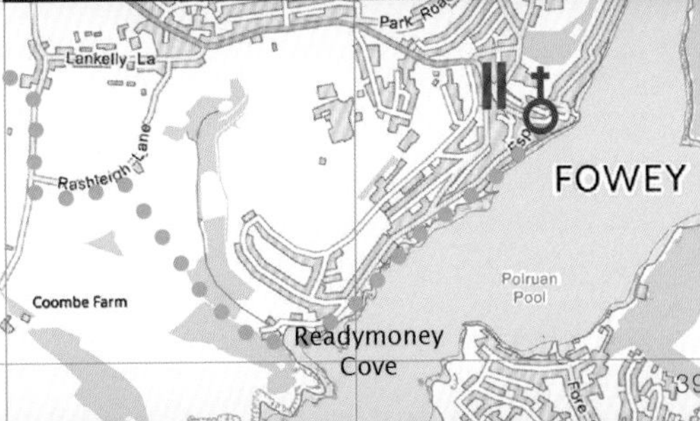

Fowey

Fowey

Novelists Daphne du Maurier and Kenneth Grahame were inspired by Fowey. Here Kenneth Grahame found the inspiration for *'The Wind in the Willows'*, his popular tales and exploits of Mole, Water Rat and Toad. In the book the Water Rat tells Mole solemnly: 'Believe me, my young friend there is nothing - absolutely nothing - half so much worth doing as simply messing about in boats.'

At Fowey estuary, many enjoyable hours can be spent watching 'messing about in boats'. On leaving Fowey harbour, following the coast path, there are large-scale wicker representations of Kenneth Grahame's enchanting characters in a hotel garden.

In Medieval times, it was Polruan that was the major harbour and port for pilgrims travelling from Ireland and Wales to Santiago de Compostela in Spain.

St. Goron

St. Goron or St. Gorun first established his home in Bodmin, but moved to Fowey when St. Petroc arrived. He then set up home in a typically Celtic setting: a sheltered inlet by a stream on the hills above Fowey Church. These hills are now called Langurthowe, *'lan'* meaning *'holy'*, and *'gurthowe'* after the saint himself. However, when another saint, St. Fimbarrus arrived, he disappeared.

St. Fimbarrus

Who was St. Fimbarrus of Fowey? There are two possible candidates: St. Fimbarrus of Fowey could have been the great Finnbarr (also known as Barry), the Irish abbot and bishop, who was the founder of the leading diocese of Cork in 606. In *'The Lives of Irish Saints'*, Finnbarr was given the name *'Fionn-Barr', 'the fair-haired one'* due to his shining hair. He loved 'the solitude of the hills' and liked 'to live by lapping waters under high crags'. Two miraculous stories are associated with Finnbarr: One day whilst he was sitting under a hazel bush a visitor asked him for a visible sign that God was with him. The catkins promptly turned to nuts and fell to the ground. Another time, Christ is said to have lifted Finnbarr by the right hand to see the glory of heaven, and from that time onwards his right hand blazed with light, so much so that he had to wear gloves. In art, Finnbarr is depicted as a bishop with a branch of hazel nuts in his hand and with his right hand emitting light. Finnbarr was a great traveller, visiting the Island of Barra in the Outer Hebrides, where he founded the influential monastic centre 'Cille Bharra'.

The second candidate for St. Fimbarrus of Fowey is St. Barry, son of the Welsh King Brychan and uncle to St. Cadoc, who gave his name to Barry Island off south Wales and travelled on pilgrimage with St. David to Rome.

christian reference

They came to Capernaum. When Jesus was in the house, he asked them, 'What were you arguing about on the road?' But they kept quiet, because on the way they had argued about who was the greatest. Sitting down, Jesus called the Twelve and said, 'Anyone who wants to be first must be the very last, and the servant of all'. *(Mark 9:33-35)*

St. Paul wrote in his letter to Christians in Corinth: 'What, after all, is Apollos? And what is Paul? Only servants, through whom you came to believe- as the Lord has assigned to each his task. I planted the seed, Apollos watered it, but God has been making it grow. So neither the one who plants nor the one who waters is anything, but only God who makes things grow. The one who plants and the one who waters have one purpose, and they will each be rewarded according to their own labour. For we are fellow workers in God's service.' *(1 Corinthians 3:5-9)*

personal reflection

In *'The Wind in the Willows'* different attitudes to life are expressed by the characters. In Fowey, with so many people coming and going, there could be a clash of different approaches and endeavours. It is salutary to learn of disputes between some of Jesus' disciples, as well as in the early church in Corinth around Apollos and St. Paul, and later amongst the Celtic missionaries.

In my working life, I have often found it difficult to get on with colleagues: sometimes it's just personal chemistry not working out, but sometimes it can be over a point of principle or a different approach to tackling the latest presenting problem.

questions

As you travel on your way today, what are the conflicts within your own life? Can you find the way of reconciliation?

Readymoney Cove

personal reflection

The walk comes to the charming Readymoney Cove, which is a derivation of the Cornish *'redeman'* meaning *'stony ford'*.

I found Lankelly Woods and the arch supporting the carriage drive to Menabilly House (Daphne du Maurier's setting for '*Rebecca*' and '*My Cousin Rachel*') particularly evocative and romantic - you could almost see the carriages trundling up to the old house.

celtic crosses

In the graveyard at Tregaminion Chapel there are two Celtic crosses. The ancient people of Britain put up standing stones *(menhirs)* to mark a significant holy place like a burial ground, a place where they believed the 'membrane between heaven and earth to be thin'. Sometimes the Celtic church adapted the Druid stones for their own use. They put a round stone on top of existing standing stones. This round stone that had a cross in the centre, signified the Sun or Son of God. Tregaminion Chapel was not the original location for these crosses: one was found nearby in the stones of a footbridge across a stream in Milltown.

There are more Celtic crosses in Tywardreath churchyard. This church does not have Celtic roots but it was an important monastic centre in Medieval times: the Benedictine Priory of Black Monks.

personal reflection

The crosses can become markers, touchstones and companions for you, connecting you with the past and strengthening and encouraging you in the same way that towers or spires can on the Cornish Celtic Way. These crosses are physical way markers and reminders of faith in the landscape. You can imagine gatherings around them listening to the tales of Jesus.

action

Touch the centre of the Celtic cross as you did the centrepiece of the door at St. Germans. You could consider this as propelling you forward, drawing on the strength of the pioneering saints St. Goran or St. Fimbarrus.

personal reflection

At the top of a field there is a wonderful view over Par and St. Austell Bay where it feels as if the whole world stretches out before you and there is an expansive sense of your own possibility and potential. Soon you pass the 'CHICKS' centre, a charity which provides Children's Holidays for Inner City Kids.

questions

As you go on your journey today, uplifted by the wonderful vista and possibilities of St. Austell Bay stretching ahead of you, what opportunity can you create to enable other people to be blessed in this way? Whose horizons could you help to be expanded by a visit here?

st. blaise

The end of this section's walk is near to St. Blazey Church. St. Blaisé was the fourth century Armenian Bishop of Sebestea who was killed by the Romans. St. Blaisé is reputed to have healed sore throats: two crossed candles were held to the throat to effect the cure. On St. Blaisé feast day parishioners still cross their arms on their chest in his memory. St. Blaisé also used altar candle wax as a cure for rotten teeth.

personal reflection

I found my companions in this section of the Cornish Celtic Way at the Eden Yard Backpackers' Hostel at Tregrehan Mills, where I was warmly greeted.

chapter 5

there's something in the soil!

st. blazey - luxulyan - helman tor gate

stop off: eden project

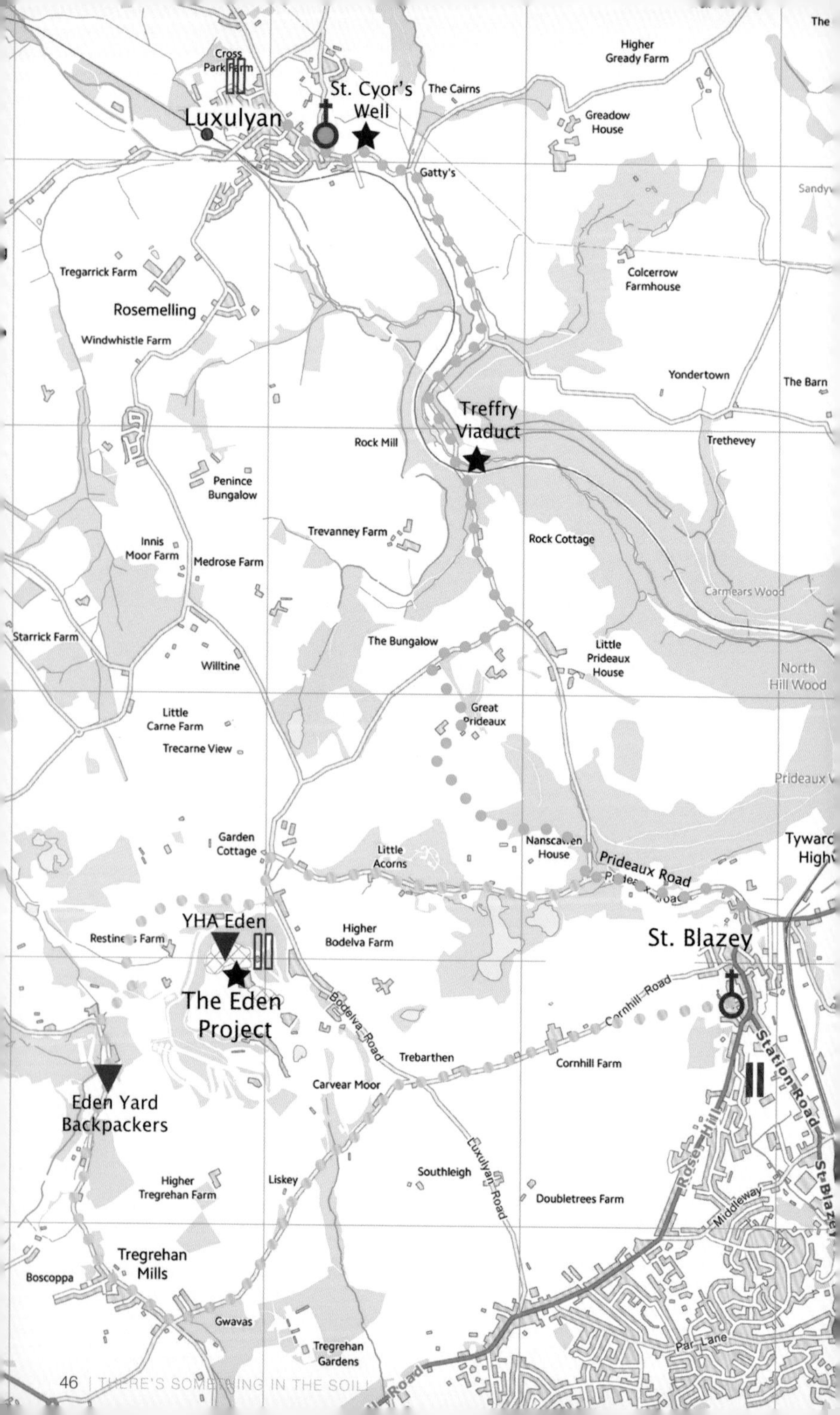
Luxulyan
St. Cyor's Well
Cross Park Farm
The Cairns
Higher Gready Farm
Greadow House
Gatty's
Tregarrick Farm
Rosemelling
Windwhistle Farm
Colcerrow Farmhouse
Yondertown
The Barn
Treffry Viaduct
Rock Mill
Trethevey
Penince Bungalow
Trevanney Farm
Rock Cottage
Innis Moor Farm
Medrose Farm
Carmears Wood
Starrick Farm
The Bungalow
Little Prideaux House
North Hill Wood
Willtine
Great Prideaux
Little Carne Farm
Trecarne View
Garden Cottage
Little Acorns
Nanscawen House
Prideaux Road
YHA Eden
Higher Bodelva Farm
St. Blazey
The Eden Project
Bodelva Road
Cornhill Road
Trebarthen
Cornhill Farm
Carvear Moor
Station Road
Eden Yard Backpackers
Rose Hill
Southleigh
Luxulyan Road
Higher Tregrehan Farm
Liskey
Doubletrees Farm
Middleway
Tregrehan Mills
Boscoppa
Gwavas
Tregrehan Gardens
Par Lane

DISTANCE: 3.5MILES/5.5KM | TIME: 2HOURS | DIFFICULTY: MODERATE

St. Blazey to Luxulyan

This includes a diversion from the Saints Way in order to visit the Treffry viaduct and aqueduct and avoid a bull! The Saints Way is rejoined at Luxulyan Church.

From St. Blazey petrol station find the Saints Way marker and cross into Prideaux Road. Take the first road right signposted to Luxulyan Valley and then look for the Saints Way sign left into the woods. At the top of the woods, follow the clear path, keeping the wood on your right. Eventually there is a stile into a field. Walk in this field with the fence/boundary on your right, to the stile in the top right hand corner. Turn right on the track, passing through the farm, and then bear left to join the road at Great Prideaux Bungalow. At the T-junction, *ignore* the Saints Way sign into the field (there is a 'Beware of the Bull' sign and likely to be cattle on the way beyond the woods) turning right along the road.

At the next junction turn left, following the narrow lane, under the railway to the Treffry Viaduct. From the Treffry Viaduct information board, climb a short distance to find an aqueduct and wide path, walk left.

To visit the top of the viaduct cross the aqueduct by the footbridge and climb the path through the wood. Return back to the aqueduct by this footbridge, continuing on the aqueduct path away from the viaduct.

Rejoin the lane just beyond the car park, continue through the valley, bearing left at the next junction into the village. Stop off at St. Cyor's Well before the steep steps up to Luxulyan Churchyard.

Diversion to Eden

To visit the Eden Project, walk from St. Blazey petrol station ignore the Saints Way sign to Prideaux Road and continue on Bridge St./Fore St. to St. Blazey Church. Turn right in front of the church up Churchfield Place on a path through fields that lead to Cornhill Farm and a lane. Walk left along this to a junction. At this junction turn right for the entrance to the Eden Project or go straight on to Tregehan Mills to find Eden Yard Backpackers' Hostel. After visiting The Eden Project, you can rejoin the Saints Way at the turning for Luxuylan Valley in Prideaux Road (see map).

the eden project

Bless the Lord all you works of the Lord:
sing his praise and exalt him forever.
Bless the Lord, you heavens:
sing his praise and exalt him forever.
Bless the Lord you angels of the Lord,
bless the Lord all his hosts,
Bless the Lord you waters above the heavens:
sing his praise and exalt him forever.
Bless the Lord all that grows in the ground:
sing his praise and exalt him forever.
Bless the Lord you springs,
bless the Lord you seas and rivers,
Bless the Lord you whales and all that swim in the waters:
sing his praise and exalt him forever.
Bless the Lord all birds of the air,
bless the Lord all beasts and cattle,
Bless the Lord all people on earth:
sing his praise and exalt him forever.

Extract from Benedicite - A Song of Creation

personal reflection - the eden project

You might want to pause your journey as I did, and stop off at the Eden Project.

The futuristic biomes of the Eden Project are an internationally renowned and hugely visited tourist attraction. It is a celebration of the natural world in all its diversity, beauty and wonder, seeking to preserve and propagate the planet's biodiversity and looking to the future as it considers the frailty of our ecosystems.

Throughout history, people have conveyed their values through the construction and veneration of grand buildings: For example, the ancient cathedrals in Medieval times were built to the glory of God. The grand shopping malls of the 1980s and 1990s were built to celebrate the dominance of commercialism and materialism and million pound football stadiums are built amongst inner-city housing. The skyline of London is now dominated by jostling and competing towers such as the Shard, Canary Wharf and the Gherkin, built to display financial power and business prestige. By contrast, Cornwall has built the Eden Project. This is not surprising as Cornwall is an area of extraordinary beauty and has Celtic roots. The Celts loved and worked within nature. I would argue that here there is something special: that these deep Celtic roots in the soil of Cornwall have enabled this great endeavour to thrive and grow. The Eden Project is truly a holy endeavour, a modern place of pilgrimage and hope for the future.

personal reflection - getting lost

Do you sometimes think you're going in the right direction, and travel for many miles along a particular course, only to realise that you've been going around in circles and you find yourself returning to the place you thought you'd left behind? This happened to me several times in this section of the Cornish Celtic Way. There are lots of confusing paths around the Eden Project, and then I got lost in a field near Prideaux House. I couldn't see the next way marker and I hastily walked around three corners of a field in a herd of unfriendly bullocks. I cut down through a wood and ended up on the same road I had left an hour before! Although I had carefully studied the map, I still went wrong. I looked at the stone I'd picked up on Downderry beach, which seemed to show that there would be lots of different roads to travel. I saw a robin and a pheasant who encouraged me on my way, despite this confusion.

This made me think about my spiritual life: of feeling that I was progressing forward when in fact I was going round in circles, trapped in a loop from which I couldn't escape. The experiences on pilgrimage helped me to break out of these old patterns and find new directions in life.

Treffry viaduct

Treffry viaduct

Treffry's immense and magnificent viaduct is made up of ten arches - the longest in Great Britain. It was built in 1839-1842 as a viaduct and an aqueduct. It carried a horse-drawn tramway, an important transport route for the china clay industry up until the early twentieth century.

personal reflection

The Treffry viaduct, like the Eden Project, is another grand human creation and achievement; it seemed to perfectly enhance Luxulyan Valley. Van Morrison in his song *'Avalon of the Heart'*, from the 1990 album *'Enlightenment'* sings of coming upon the enchanted vale by the viaduct of his dreams. I came upon it so unexpectedly that it took my breath away with its sheer scale and audacity. Local travel writer, Murray, wrote that it was a 'beautiful, romantic scene of wood and rock, indeed one of the finest, if not the finest of all Cornish valleys'. The Celts believed that vales and rivers were holy and sacred spaces and I encountered that here in Luxulyan Valley.

St. Sulian

St. Sulian was born in the sixth century, the son of the Welsh King of Powys, Brucemail. He abandoned his royal heritage and renounced his lineage for the religious life, having to overcome some violent parental opposition. Together with St. Samson and other Welsh monks, St. Sulian travelled through Cornwall to Brittany. In Brittany, there is a place called 'Lossulian' founded by St. Sulian.

luxulyan church

Luxulyan, is derived from *'lan sulian'* meaning *'the holy place of St. Sulian'*. The circular elevated site of the church suggests that it was formerly a communal burial place, a pre-Christian holy site. St. Sulian established a home and Celtic cell here. Luxulyan was linked to the monks of Tywardreath. In 1412 Luxulyan Church was rededicated by returning Medieval crusaders to St. Cyricacus and St. Julitta. St. Julitta was a widow killed with her three year-old son, St. Cyricacus, at Tarsus in 304.

st. cyor's well

St. Cyor's well is just below Luxuylan Church. It was originally a sacred well which was Christianised by the Celtic Christians. The well was restored and surrounded by a well house in 1412 and later was drained of its source by the construction of the railway. St. Cyor was an Irish saint, of whom there is little in recorded history. Some historians prefer a later medieval tradition that suggests the well name is a derivation of St. Cyricacus.

christian reference

Jesus said: 'Anyone who loves their father or mother more than me is not worthy of me... Whoever does not take up their cross and follow me is not worthy of me... Whoever loses their life for my sake will find it. Anyone who welcomes you, welcomes me... If anyone gives even a cup of cold water to one of these little ones who is my disciple, truly I tell you, that person will certainly not lose their reward.' *(Matthew 10:37-42)*

personal reflection

I found Luxulyan Church to be a very prayerful and welcoming place, with the Saints Way pilgrim stamp and refreshments. This area of my pilgrimage seemed to focus on water- the stream, the drink, the holy well and the aqueduct.

St. Sulian came up against opposition when he left home for his faith. When I was planning my pilgrimage one person wanted to know who was paying for it, and another saw me as abandoning my work. I was however very fortunate that many people actively encouraged me and blessed me in my exploration of the Cornish Celtic Way, providing me with prayers, words of encouragement and a pilgrim's walking staff.

questions

Who opposes you? What resistance have you had to overcome to start this journey?

DISTANCE: 3MILES/5KM | TIME: 1.5HOURS | DIFFICULTY: EASY

Luxulyan to Helman Tor Gate

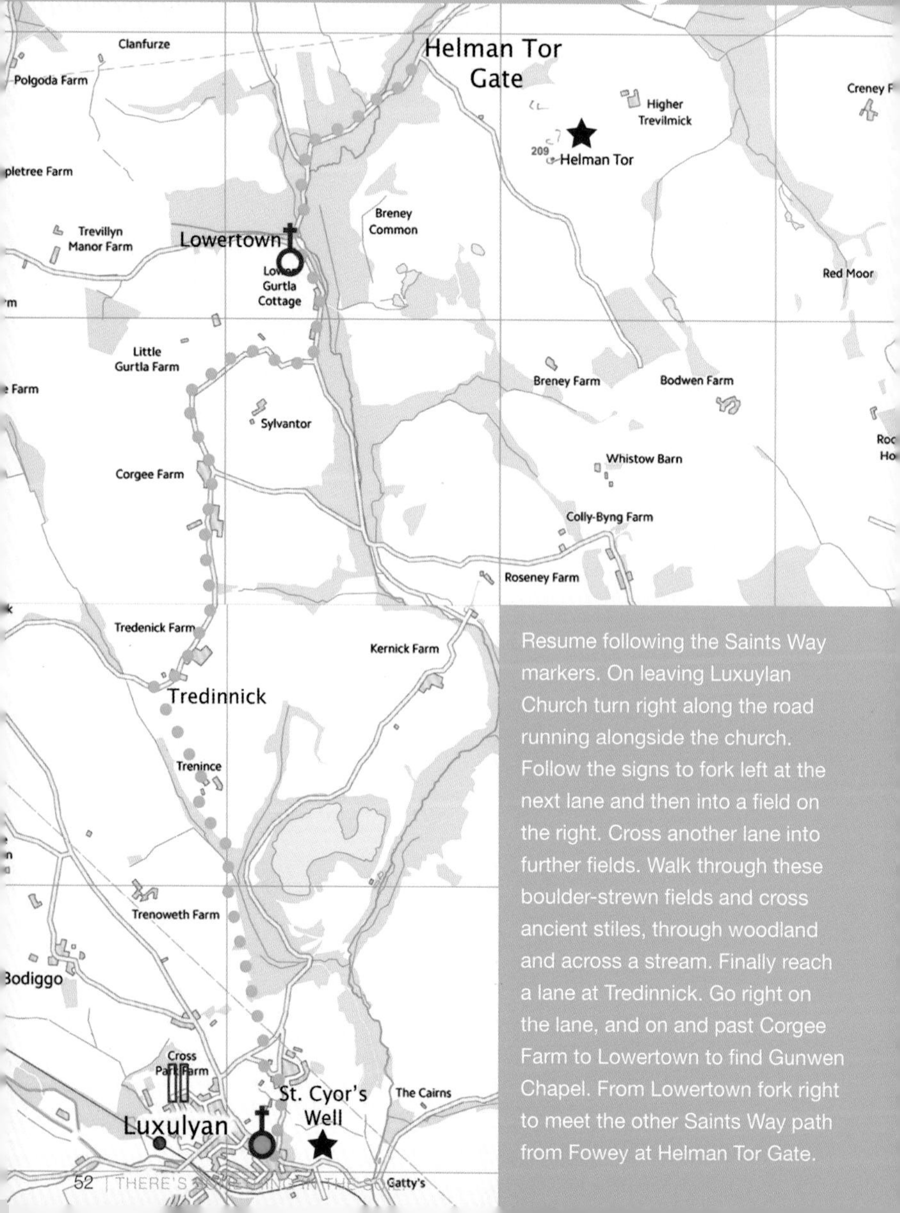

Resume following the Saints Way markers. On leaving Luxuylan Church turn right along the road running alongside the church. Follow the signs to fork left at the next lane and then into a field on the right. Cross another lane into further fields. Walk through these boulder-strewn fields and cross ancient stiles, through woodland and across a stream. Finally reach a lane at Tredinnick. Go right on the lane, and on and past Corgee Farm to Lowertown to find Gunwen Chapel. From Lowertown fork right to meet the other Saints Way path from Fowey at Helman Tor Gate.

action

Touch the cross at Luxulyan churchyard gate. It is made from local volcanic rock, luxulyanite. Although now in the churchyard, it was found being used as a gatepost in the early part of the nineteenth century. After you leave Luxulyan village and walk along the boggy path with its ancient granite stiles on the way to Tredinnick, imagine that you are treading an ancient way, maybe along the very paths taken by St. Sulian and his companions. These paths were rediscovered in 1984 by Cliff Townes and Alf Fooks who went on to establish 'The Saints Way'.

gunwen chapel, lowertown

A huge Christian revival took place in Cornwall at the beginning of the nineteenth century, bringing about a simpler and more direct version of Christianity which led to small chapels springing up in villages all over Cornwall. Initially, this movement was Methodist, led by evangelists John and Charles Wesley. William O'Bryan became a Christian and went on to found the Bible Christians, a more radical version of the movement. He was born in a nearby farm and set up Gunwen Chapel. As a child, O'Bryan had been blessed by Wesley with the words: 'May he be a blessing to hundreds and thousands'. In the tradition of the Celtic saints, O'Bryan travelled extensively and dedicated himself to a life spreading Christianity. O'Bryan said: 'I felt a deep sense of duty laid on me to seek the wandering souls of men'. The Methodist Society gave funds to O'Bryan to build Gunwen Chapel but he didn't want to be tied down and travelled as far as America in his preaching mission. As a result of this, he was rejected by Methodism. O'Bryan had the same freedom of spirit as the Celtic saints. There's something in the soil!

blessed
are those
whose
strength
is in you,
whose
hearts
are set on
pilgrimage.

psalm 84:5

chapter 6

being alive to the signs

helman tor gate - lanivet - withiel

DISTANCE: 3MILES/5KM | TIME: 1.5HOURS | DIFFICULTY: EASY

helman tor gate to lanivet

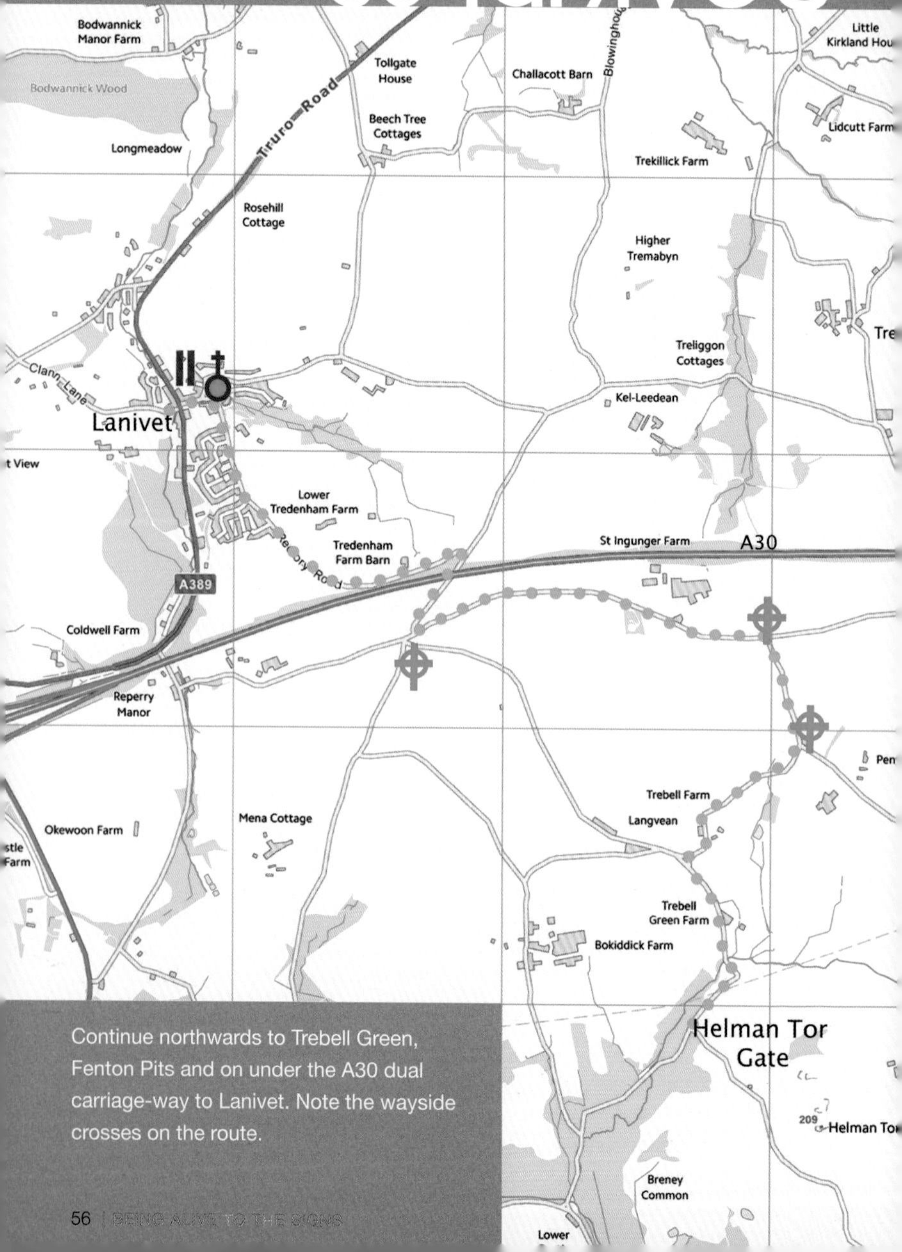

Continue northwards to Trebell Green, Fenton Pits and on under the A30 dual carriage-way to Lanivet. Note the wayside crosses on the route.

wayside crosses and way markers

Some crosses on this part of the route are:

fenton pits cross

The top of the cross was restored in the 1920s by the workers of Lanhydrock House.

st. ingunger cross

To mark an important early Christian centre where there was a chapel and holy well.

'v.t lani' way marker

The symbolism on this way marker could be a hand pointing the way to Lanivet or the scallop shell used in a similar way on St. Michael's Way as a sign of the way to Santiago de Compostela.

lanivet churchyard

Two crosses, one of which is a wheel-head cross with a unusual carved figure of a man with a tail.

They asked Jesus: Are you the one who is to come, or should we expect someone else?

(Matthew 11:3)

personal reflection

Any person following a route may study the map and the environment carefully, scan the horizon, and look out for the next path. There isn't one particular saint to focus on at this stage of the Cornish Celtic Way, but there are many signs that they walked these paths - the huge number of way markers and Celtic crosses. I gradually realised that the presence of a church tower or spire on the skyline gave me a great sense of blessing, not just because they were places of destination and arrival, but because they indicated to me that the very land I was walking on was blessed and had been walked by many others before me. I found this to be especially true as I walked the long road from Lanivet when I was greatly uplifted to see Withiel Church on the horizon. Similarly, the wayside crosses became great sources: they energised me, propelled me forward, and lead me on with hope and encouragement. Pilgrimage writer, John Key, wrote that 'the stone crosses stand in silent tribute as they have stood for hundreds and hundreds of years'. Where they were planted in the ground maybe a saint had preached, died, or healed, or maybe the crosses were placed to mark territory and claim the land for God. Maybe they were used to mark the place of a sacred tree.

lanivet

Lanivet means *'lan'* holy place and *'ivet'* could indicate *'sacred grove'* or a saint's name. The saint at Lanivet could be St. Nivet, who was the daughter of St. Brychan of Wales, St. Nevet, a nun from Lannevet in Brittany or St. Ivo or St. Ia. Apart from St. Ia, little is known of these saints. Lanivet Church was restored by James Piers St. Aubyn in 1865. There are ten Celtic crosses in Lanivet parish besides the two in the churchyard indicating the importance of Lanivet in Celtic times. Close to Lanivet church is St. Benet's Abbey, the English home of a military order, the *'Hospitallers'*, founded in 1144 to care for sick pilgrims on the way to Santiago de Compostela; it is now a B&B. The ruins of a Medieval chapel are to be found in its grounds. Lanivet marks the half-way point of the Saints Way, and is also geographically at the centre of Cornwall.

poem

The Romans built straight roads
held the high ground
took no detours
saw alien eyes hostile
hidden places traps.

Holy men like meandering streams
sought the easiest route
skirting the rocks and boggy ground
embracing the unexpected
finding men good.

Celtic saint and consul
each left their mark
statute and law
order and control
dreams, vision and song
glimpses of immortality
all woven into the fabric of this land.
(Jenna Plewes, 'Legacy' from her book 'Gifts' used by kind permission.)

DISTANCE: 3.75MILES/6KM | TIME: 2HOURS | DIFFICULTY: EASY

lanivet to withiel

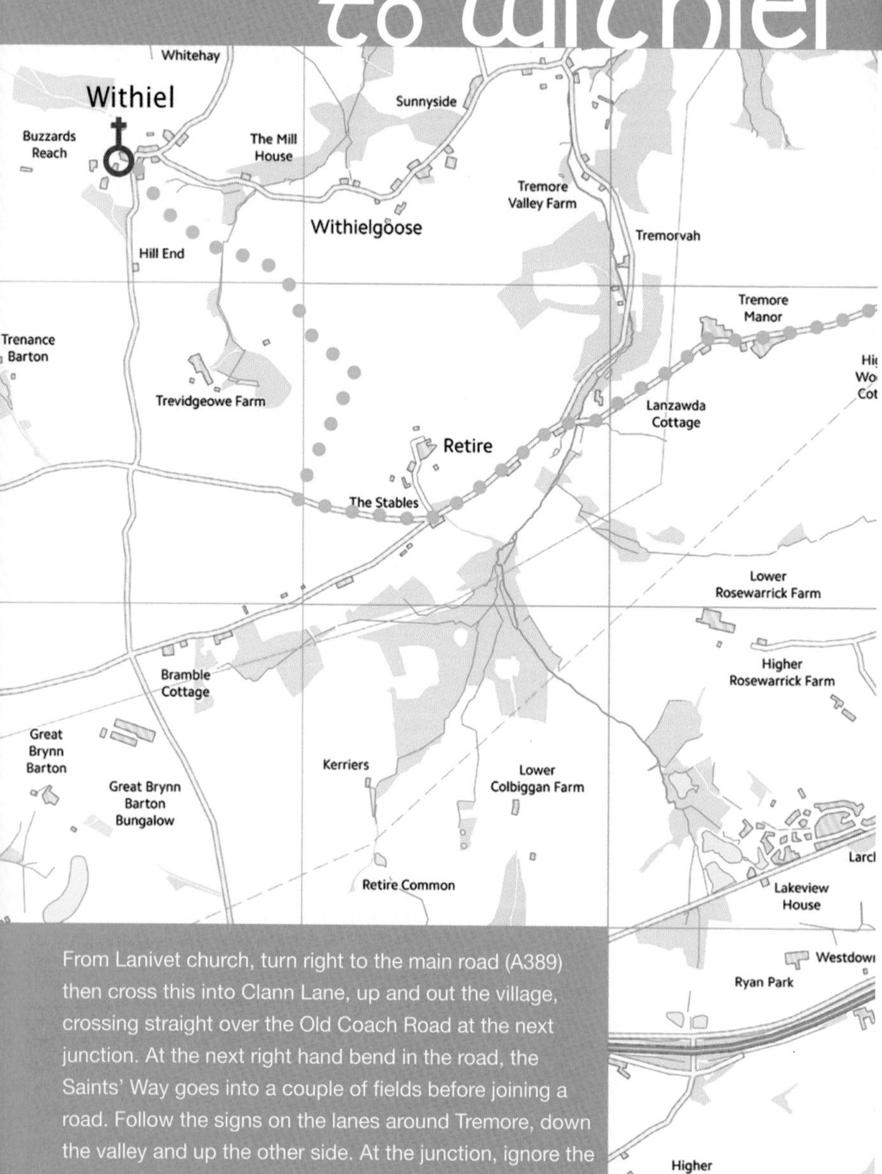

From Lanivet church, turn right to the main road (A389) then cross this into Clann Lane, up and out the village, crossing straight over the Old Coach Road at the next junction. At the next right hand bend in the road, the Saints' Way goes into a couple of fields before joining a road. Follow the signs on the lanes around Tremore, down the valley and up the other side. At the junction, ignore the road to 'Retire' on the right, but take the next right. After about 600 yards, take the next lane from this road (right) and then a left over fields crossing a valley to Withiel.

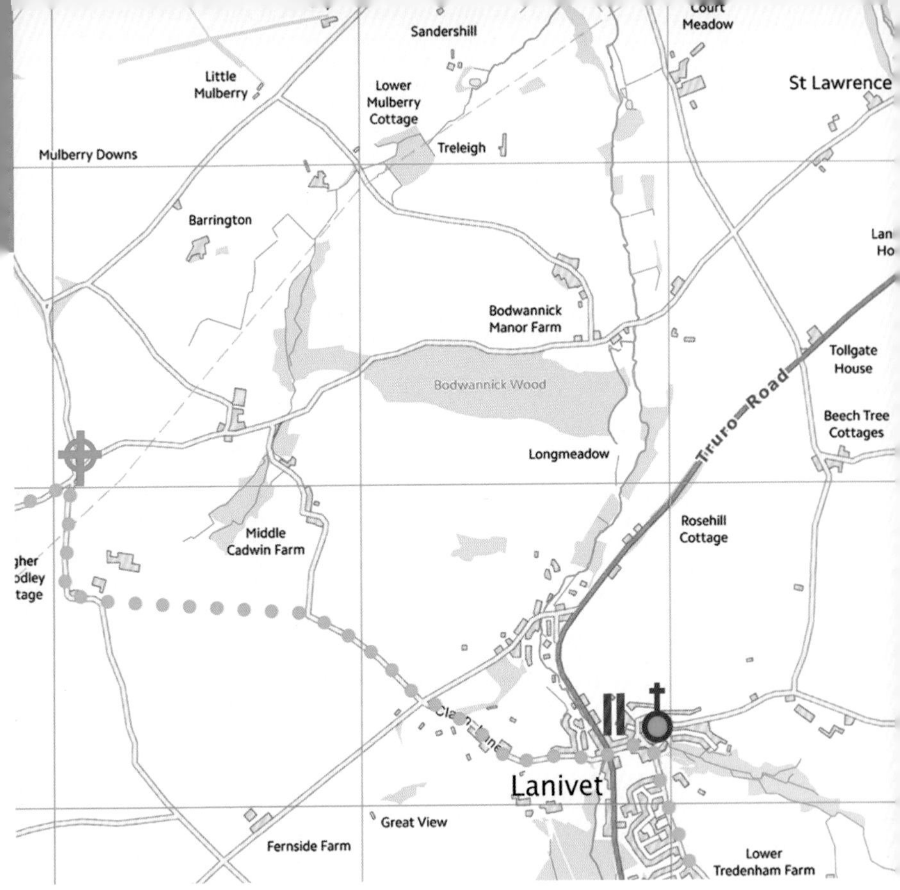

personal reflection

Today I was encouraged by a stoat. On the way to Withiel, I came to a flooded path which seemed to stretch as far as I could see. If I went through it I would have been up to my knees in water. As I was considering what to do, a stoat appeared and showed me that a way had been created along the top of the hedge. I thanked God for the appearance of the stoat at this moment. I later crossed my first ford at Tregustick and I thanked God for those who had created the way across the water. In the boggy areas, I also found that someone had put down tree logs on which to walk. I reflected that people themselves can be way markers, guiding and encouraging others in the way that they live their lives. It is also important to have way markers for the passage of time. Life is marked by occasions and festivals such as Christmas, Easter, harvest, birthdays, anniversaries and holidays; the celebration of which is vital to mark the way through life.

lanzota valley

As you cross the fields to Withiel, you go through a valley called *'lanzota'*, *'lan'* meaning *'holy'* and *'zota'* could be the saints name *'Zota'*. This could be the site of an original Celtic settlement.

There was a stunted handpost just on the crest,
Only a few feet high:
She was tired, and we stopped in the twilight-time for her rest,
At the crossroads close thereby.

She leant back, being so weary, against its stem,
And laid her arms out on its own,
Each open palm stretched out to each end of them,
Her sad face sideways thrown.

Her white-clothed form at this dim-lit cease of day
Made her look as one crucified
In my gaze at her from the midst of the dusty way,
And hurriedly "Don't", I cried.

I do not think she heard. Loosing thence she said,
As she stepped forth ready to go; I am rested now. Something strange came into my head;
I wish I hadn't leant so.

Thomas Hardy, Near Lanivet, 1872

chapter 7

companions on the way

withiel - st. breock downs - st. issey - padstow

DISTANCE: 3MILES/5KM | TIME: 1.5HOURS | DIFFICULTY: MODERATE

Withiel to St. Breock Downs

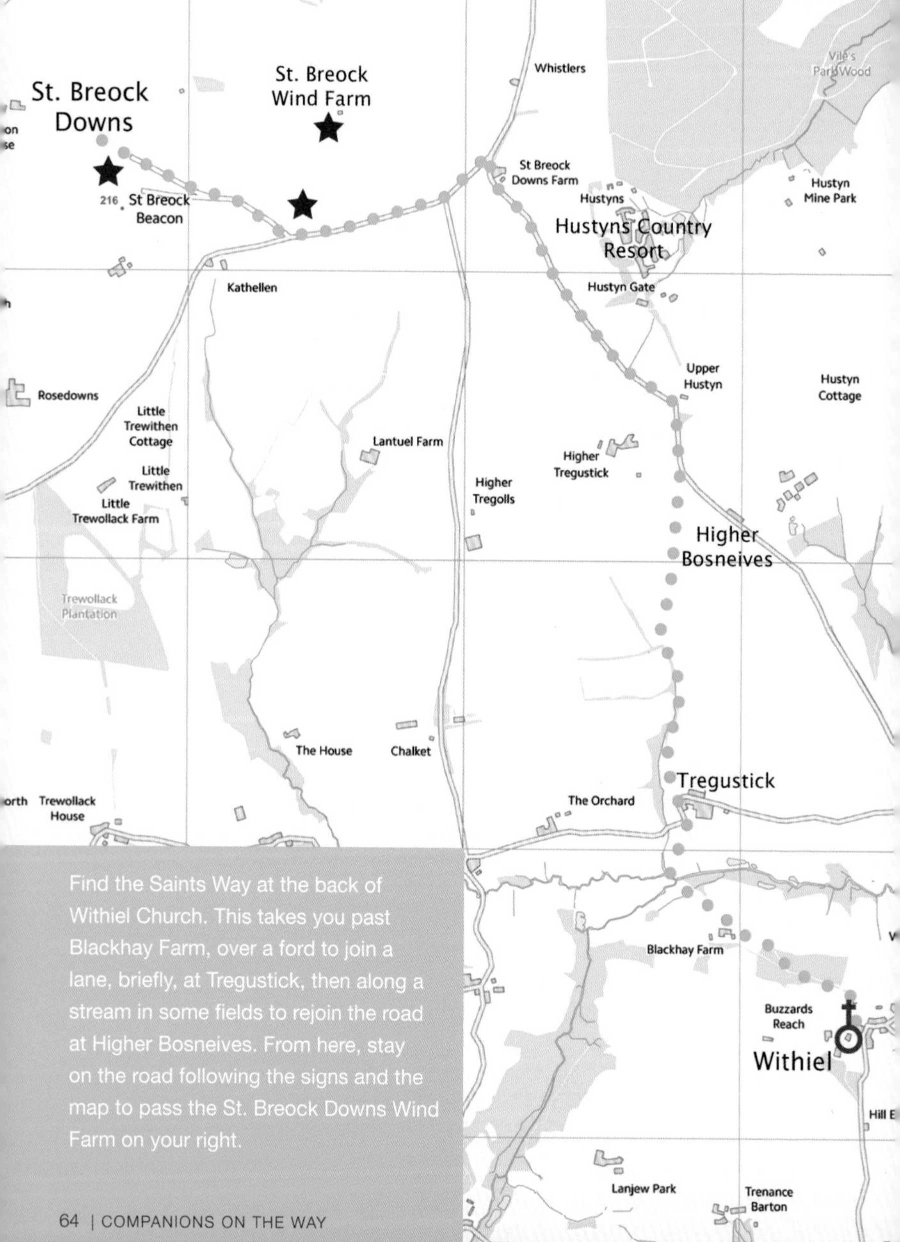

Find the Saints Way at the back of Withiel Church. This takes you past Blackhay Farm, over a ford to join a lane, briefly, at Tregustick, then along a stream in some fields to rejoin the road at Higher Bosneives. From here, stay on the road following the signs and the map to pass the St. Breock Downs Wind Farm on your right.

withiel church

Withiel Church is dedicated to St. Clement who was killed in Crimea by being chained to an anchor and thrown into the sea. (St. Clement lived in Rome in the first century). He became the patron saint of seafarers, whose emblem is the anchor. However, the name 'Withiel' speaks of a Celtic foundation: it may be derived from *'Wydhal'* which means *'Irishman of Gael'*.
The Saints Way guide describes Withiel Church as 'attractive, spacious and light'. It is a Georgian-style church which was restored by the last Prior of Bodmin before the Dissolution of the Monasteries. There is also a grand rectory next door, built in 1520 by Prior Thomas Veryan.

standing stones at st. breock downs

There is a very steep climb from Tregustick to Higher Bosneives and up to St. Breock Wind Farm. An ancient settlement was established around the St. Breock standing stones. There is a 'long-stone' here dating from the Bronze Age which, at the weight of 16.5 tonnes, is the heaviest standing stone in Cornwall. Since Medieval times, it has been used as a meeting place, and is called '*men gurta*': '*stone of waiting*'. For centuries generations have made their lives here and used this high point as a look-out post. A sixteenth-century topographer, John Norden, wrote that the parish of Withiel was: 'a parish whereof there are manie (burial hills) of Romish, Saxon and Danish warrs'.

personal reflection

Our lives are put into perspective by engaging with the stories of ancient people and history, many of whose practices, rituals and lifestyles are lost to us in time.
St. Breock Downs still stands as a look-out post over the surrounding countryside, but now has a wind farm pointing our direction to the future.
It has become clear that we need to find new sources for the creation of power: for environmental reasons, to create peace and to provide energy self-sufficiency. The developed world's dependence upon the continued supply of 'black gold', fuels the arms trade and has lead to travesties such as the Iraq War, which contributed to the destabilisation of the Middle East.

st. breock

St. Breock (Breoc or Brioc) was born in Dyfed, Cardiganshire in West Wales. A credible eleventh century book, a *'Life'*, contains many accounts of St. Breock's miracles and he is the patron saint of purse makers, as a result of his many acts of charity and mercy. His parents were said to be generous, offering an open three-day feast at the start of each year. An angel is said to have instructed them to send him to St. Germanus, Bishop of Auxerre in Brittany, where he met St. Patrick and St. Illtyd. On meeting St. Germanus, a dove hovered over his head. St. Breock returned to Wales to convert his parents to Christianity, and then lead a group of 168 friends and disciples across Cornwall via 'the Saints Way' to Brittany, maybe staying in Wadebridge where St. Breock Church is dedicated to him. In Brittany, St. Breock founded a Breton monastery, where now stands an impressive cathedral at St. Brieuc. He left the monastery in the care of his nephew, St. Tudy, who may have travelled with St. Breock through Cornwall. St. Tudy is also known as a village close to Wadebridge and is himself a respected Breton saint.

song

Spirit of God, as strong as the wind,
gentle as is the dove,
give us your joy, give us your peace,
show us Jesus' love.
You inspired them, long, long ago,
They then proclaimed your word;
we see their lives serving us all:
Through them your voice is heard.
Without your help, we fail our Lord,
we cannot live His way,
we need your power,
we need your strength,
following Christ each day.
(Margaret V. Old, 1932-2001)

christian reference

Jesus said: 'The wind blows wherever it pleases. You hear its sound, but you cannot tell where it comes from or where it is going. So it is with everyone born of the Spirit'. *(John 3:8)*

In the story of the coming of the Holy Spirit 'suddenly a sound like the blowing of a violent wind came from heaven and filled the whole house where they were sitting'. *(Acts 2:2)*

questions

Where does your source of energy come from? Is it from your own self-motivation? Is it ego-driven? Do you get it from having time-off or by visiting health spas such as the 'Hustyns Country Resort'? Is all power self-generated or can we receive something of God's power in our lives?

In the mountains everything came good in me, its contours, its colours, its water, rocks, flowers and birds, it is a Journey into Being as I penetrated more deeply the mountain's life, I penetrated more deeply into my own.

Nan Shepherd

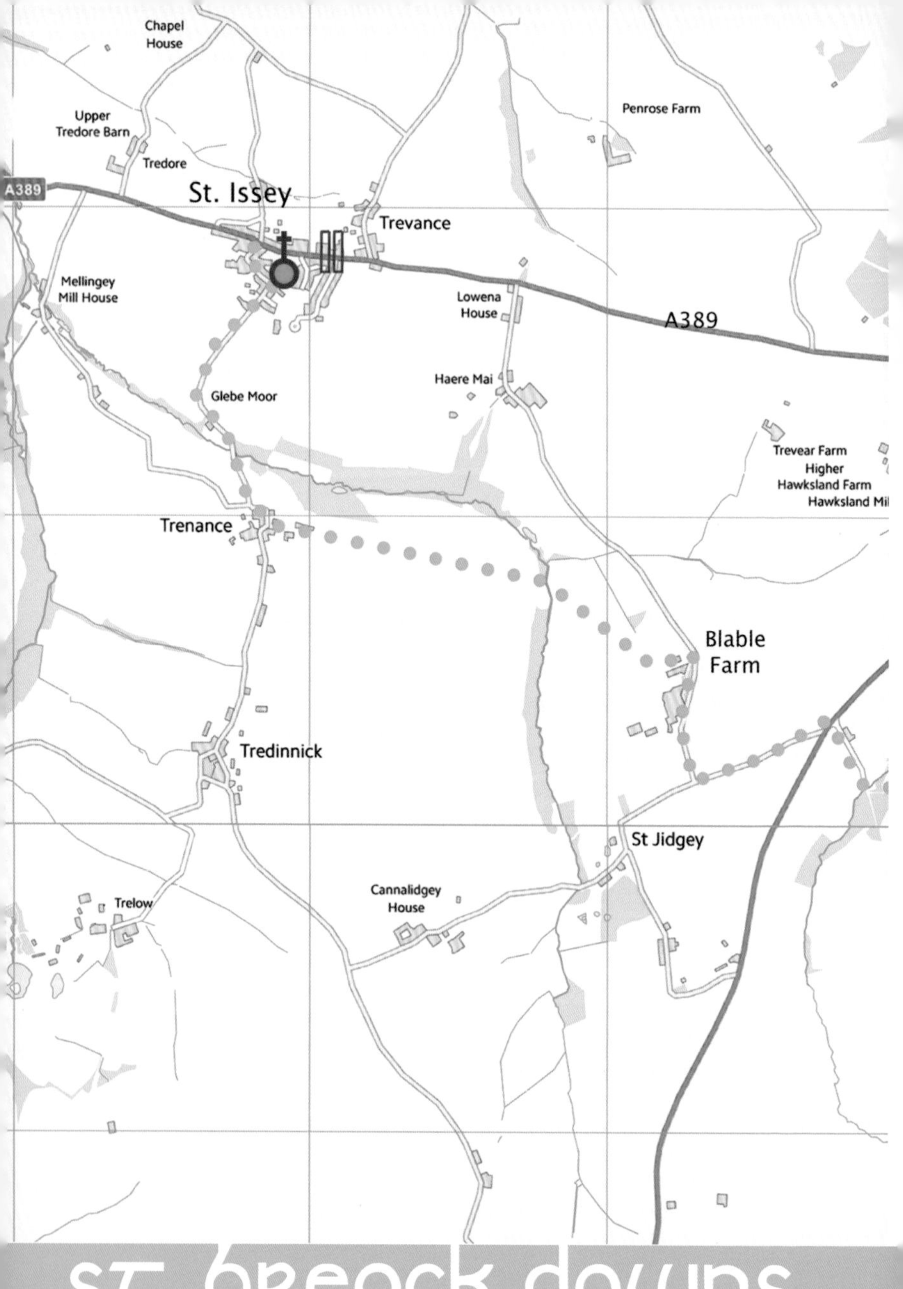

st. breock downs to st. issey

DISTANCE: 4.5MILES/7KM | TIME: 2.25HOURS | DIFFICULTY: EASY

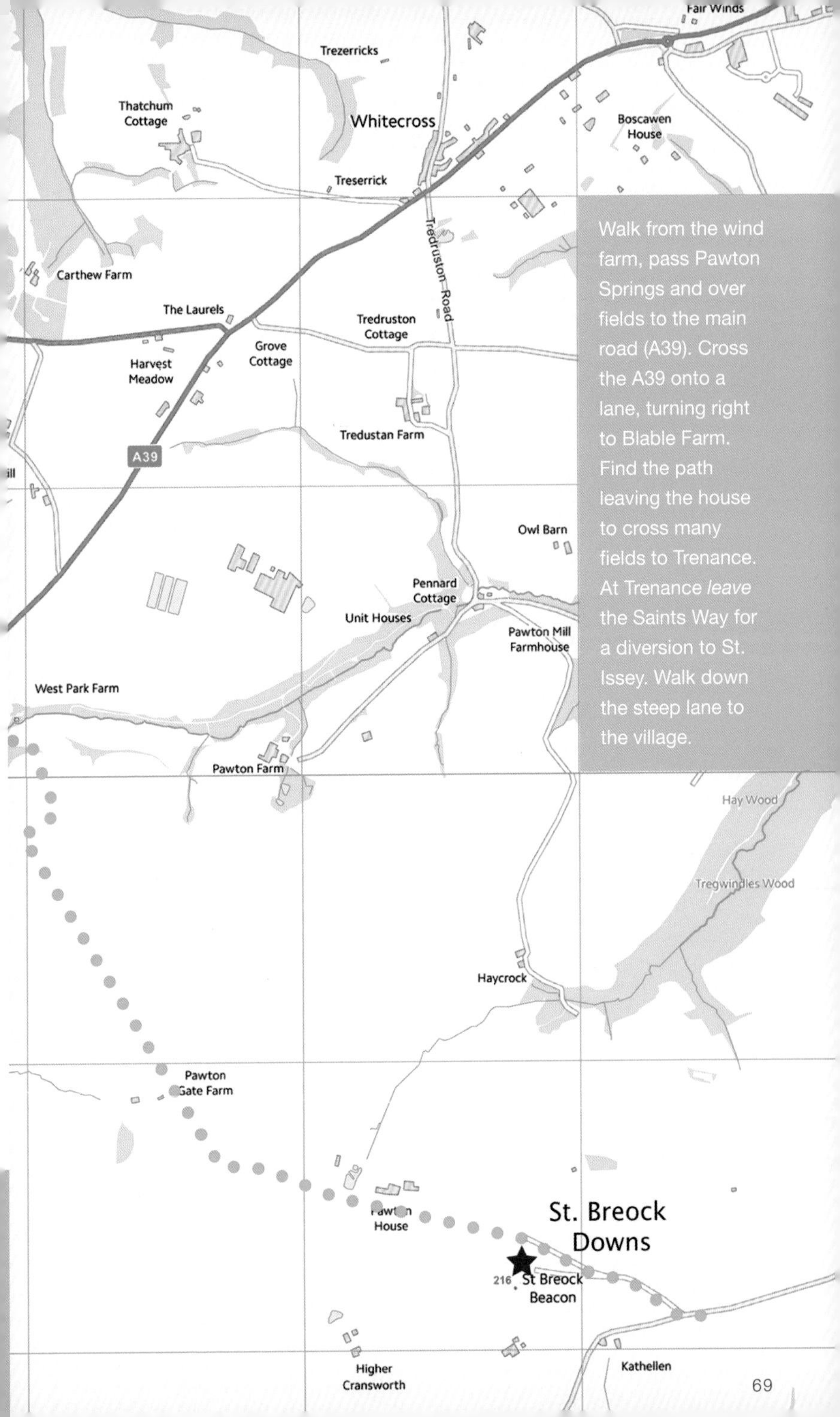

Walk from the wind farm, pass Pawton Springs and over fields to the main road (A39). Cross the A39 onto a lane, turning right to Blable Farm. Find the path leaving the house to cross many fields to Trenance. At Trenance *leave* the Saints Way for a diversion to St. Issey. Walk down the steep lane to the village.

st. issey church

st. issey church

The original church was built on this site in 600-700 and belonged to the bishop and monks of Bodmin. In Cornish, *'egloscruk'* means *'the church by a barrow'* or *'the church on a sepulchral tumulus'* or *'on the little mound'*. There are a number of pre-historic remains in the area. The settlement near Trenance was the ancient settlement of 'Blable': *'blyth-poll'* meaning *'wolf pit'*, suggesting that ancient travellers underwent dangerous journeys.

St. Issey Church was restored between 1980-1992, and is a very well-kept church, with fine stonework. *'The Church Trails'* card for St. Issey Church describes it as having 'brightness, warmth and quality'.

st. issey

Rev S. Baring Gould's book, *'Life of St. Issey'* says that St. Issey was born in 480, and was the child of the Welsh King Brychan. Brychan's children all became saints except one, who apparently lived a disparate life. St. Issey was baptised with the name *'dairdre'* meaning *'an insatiable desire for the living water of Heavenly Truth'*. (She is also known as St. Itha and St. Ida.) She is said to have been a person of tact, perception and broad-mindedness who performed miracles, had the gift of prophecy and wrote a song to the infant Jesus. When she was prioress of a community of nuns in County Limerick who ran a school for boys, she became foster mother to the iconic Celtic Christian traveller, St. Brendan the Navigator *(486-575)*. St. Brendan asked St. Issey what three things she thought were the most pleasing to God. St. Issey said they were resignation to the divine will, simplicity and large heartedness. She also said that what was most hateful to God was churlishness, love of evil, greed or gain. In art, St. Issey is depicted wearing the robe of an Irish abbess. She may not, however, have visited Cornwall in person. St. Dagan (who was a nephew of St. Petroc) may have asked St. Issey to send some of the nuns to teach Christianity in Cornwall, and they may then have dedicated this church to her as well that at Mevagissey on the south coast of Cornwall. Other stories recount that St. Issey may indeed have been brought across from Ireland by St. Petroc.

song

In Cornish land went forth her fame,
Padstow to Mevagissey,
Men saw her thirst and changed her
name. From Dorothy to Issey.
She thirsted for the stream of life,
Which from the Lamb's throne floweth,
A child she nursed, though ne'er a wife,
As in her song she showeth.
(Verses from a hymn sung at St. Issey Feast to the Irish tune St. Columba.)

personal reflection

St. Issey's large-heartedness, her companionship with many other Celtic saints and her encouragement of St. Brendan are the aspects of her life to which I feel most drawn. I reflected upon how it so important in life to welcome, pause, and encourage people, because we only live for a short while. Here I was encouraged by many: a landlady who gave me her blessing, the cheery farmer just going to work, the lady who showed me *'The Church Trails'* book at St. Issey Church (which determined the next part of the journey), the former ferryboat man, the two ladies at Little Petherick Church talking about the beauty of the forest, the Midlands couple who I met on the cliff path and finally the lady who came out of her house to encourage me up the hill to Padstow! 'Meeting people puts our lives in perspective: we are not all important or at the centre of everything, but are an integral part in the community of ordinary folk', spiritual writer Daniel O'Leary says. We are all interconnected and interdependent and once we realise this we can only feel compassion for our fellow travellers on life's journey. The mystic, Thomas Merton, talks of 'his heart being close to bursting in love for everyone around him'. This sense of oneness can heal the wounds of our isolation and separation from each other.

christian reference

To those that I meet - make me a blessing.
As I walk down the street - make me a blessing.
At work and at home - make me a blessing.
Wherever I roam - make me a blessing.
(David Adam, 'The Open Gate')

We are pilgrims on a journey,
and companions on the road;
we are here to help each other
walk the mile and bear the load.
(Extract taken from the song 'Brother, sister let me serve you' by Richard A. M. Gillard, b.1953 Copyright(c) Thankyou Music)

question

Who has blessed you on your journey today?

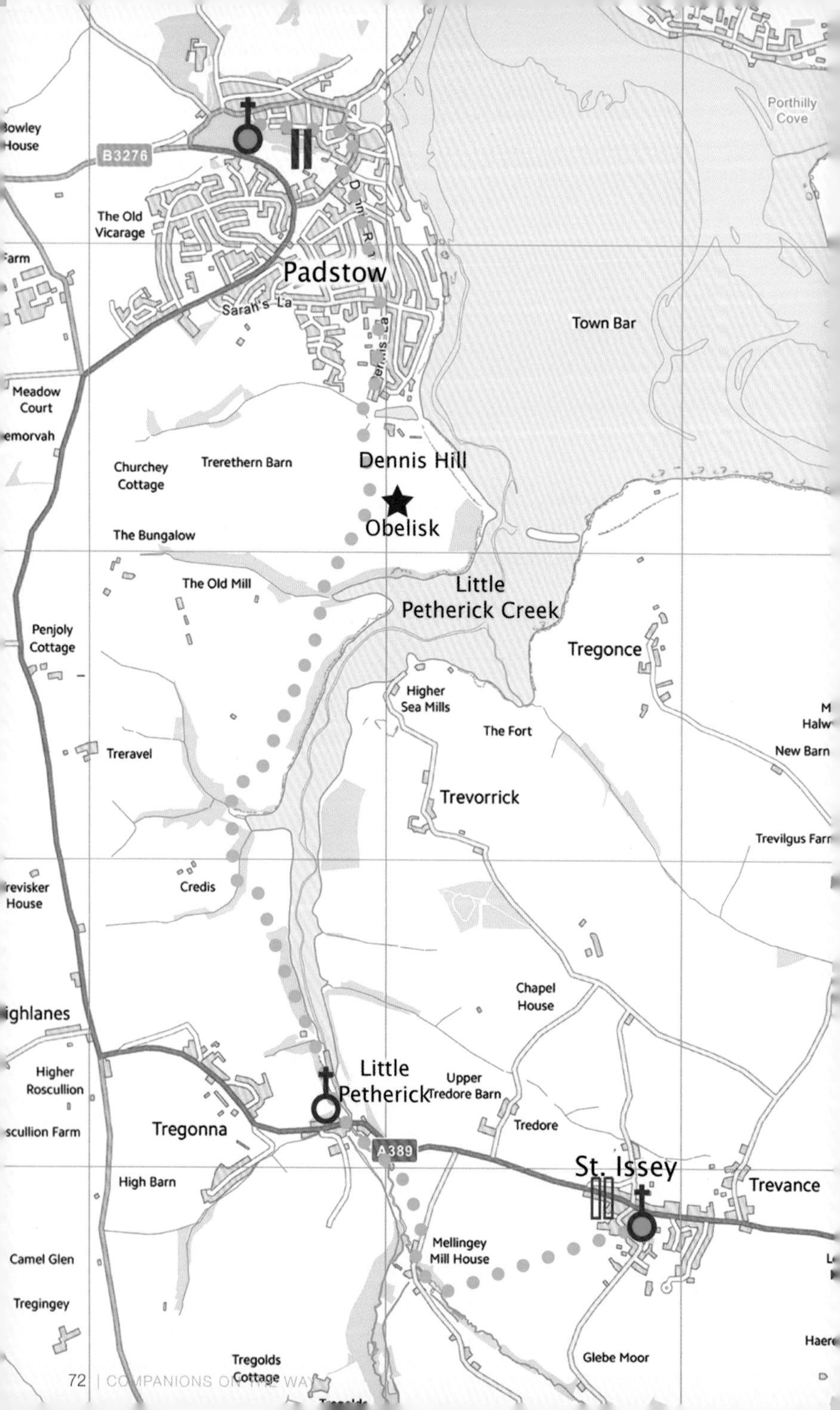
Porthilly Cove
B3276
The Old Vicarage
Padstow
Sarah's La
Town Bar
Meadow Court
Dennis Hill
Churchey Cottage
Trerethern Barn
Obelisk
The Bungalow
The Old Mill
Little Petherick Creek
Penjoly Cottage
Tregonce
Higher Sea Mills
The Fort
New Barn
Treravel
Trevorrick
Credis
Chapel House
Higher Roscullion
Little Petherick
Upper Tredore Barn
Tregonna
Tredore
A389
St. Issey
Trevance
High Barn
Mellingey Mill House
Camel Glen
Tregingey
Tregolds Cottage
Glebe Moor

DISTANCE: 3MILES/5KM | TIME: 1.25HOURS | DIFFICULTY: EASY

St. Issey to Padstow

Find the footpath opposite St. Issey Church, as shown on the map, across a valley and some fields and up to the lane at Higher Mellingey. Here you rejoin the Saints Way. Turn right and follow the lane to Mellingey after which the Saints Way path goes left into fields and down to Little Petherick.

After Little Petherick Church, the path continues between the church and the church hall. Follow the Saints Way signs along the estuary to Padstow. As you are coming in from the estuary and fields into Padstow, head for the granite Obelisk on Dennis Hill, erected in 1887 to commemorate Queen Victoria's Jubilee.

Little Petherick Church

Little Petherick is also known as St. Petroc Minor and the church was finely restored as a shrine of the Anglo-Catholic movement by Athelstan Riley in 1898. It has an interesting and impressively ornate interior.

St. Petroc

On feast days, up until the Reformation in England in the sixteenth century, the '*Lives*' of the saints were read out. After the Reformation this practice stopped but the '*Lives*' of the saints remained preserved in Brittany and as a result there exists a good record of St. Petroc in the '*Life of St. Petroc*' and in the '*Life of St. Cadoc*': 'As a pilgrim too, St. Petroc arrived at last, by the will of God in the land of the Cornishmen.'

St. Petroc was St. Cadoc's uncle and a Welsh nobleman, educated in an Irish monastery for twenty years. He set out with a small group of companions - Croidan/Credan, Medan and a woman called Dagan/Dachan/Dechana - to teach the Christian faith. They came ashore to Cornwall in their coracles, landing on the coast at Trebetherick, near Polzeath in 518. On arrival, St. Petroc took over St. Gwethinoc's earlier mission in Padstow and the town's name changed from 'Lanwethinoc' to 'Petroc's Stow'.

They established a monastic cell, school, library, infirmary and farm around the site of the present church in Padstow. St. Petroc also established an oratory and a mill at Nanceventon close to Little Petherick Church. In later life, St. Petroc established his third settlement based on the mission of St. Samson and St. Goran. At first it was a small hermitage at Bosvenegh or Bothmena (meaning '*the dwelling or abode of the monks*') which grew to become the town of Bodmin. The three significant places in St. Petroc's life (Padstow, Little Petherick and Bodmin) used to be linked on his feast day, and at one time parishioners would gather on this day at St. Breock Downs beacon for a sermon.

For those wanting to over romanticise

the Celtic saints, St. Petroc followed the Celtic practice of extreme asceticism. A Celtic monk's life involved hard physical labour and acts of penitence: St. Petroc is said to have spent many hours up to his neck in the waters of Little Petherick Creek reciting psalms every day. Celtic Christians believed that the power of evil was tangible: wrestling demons and engaging in 'spiritual warfare' and St. Petroc was said to have rid the land of an enormous serpent, kept to punish criminals by the notorious, late King Teudar. The monks kept to a frugal diet. St. Petroc is said to have only eaten barley bread, adding pulses to his diet on Sundays. St. Winwalloe (according to Wrdistan's '*Life of St. Winwalloe*') slept on a hard bed with a stone as a pillow, adding cheese but 'no flesh of animal or bird' at the weekends to his barley bread diet. His Celtic rule was considered 'too severe' and was abandoned at his monastery in Landevenec, Brittany in 818. St. David's regime at his monastery at Medevia in Wales was equally harsh and described by the contemporary historian Gildas to be 'ridiculous' and 'inhuman' for the strict water and vegetarian diet and the use of monks in place of oxen to carry the yoke.

St. Petroc had an affinity for animals. When he travelled to India he is said to have lived on an island for seven years fed miraculously by a single fish and he is depicted with his tame wolf in statues. The nearby farm named 'Blable' means 'wolf pit'. There is a statue in the sanctuary at the front of Little Petherick Church and another is brought out for Sunday services in Padstow. St. Petroc is said to have removed a splinter from a dragon's eye and to have converted the Celtic King Constantine to Christianity when a deer that escaped from a royal hunt lay down at St. Petroc's feet.

St. Petroc, like many of the Celtic saints, followed the example of the earlier Egyptian and Syrian Desert Fathers, and he lived isolated in the hermitage at Bodmin Moor into his old age. St. Petroc died on 4 June 564 at Treravel Farm. This is St. Petroc's Feast Day. A spring at the farm is said to cure sore eyes and internal illnesses.

The historian, Doble, records twenty-one churches dedicated to St. Petroc in Devon (which is more than those in Cornwall). He is also remembered in place names in Wales and Brittany.

personal reflection

Padstow has become famous due to the TV celebrity chef Rick Stein. The town has gone through a number of name changes in its history and now maybe another one: due to the number of properties, outlets and eateries owned by Rick, the town is jokingly renamed 'Padstein' by local residents.

chapter 8

Treasured finds

padstow - St. Merryn - Constantine Bay

DISTANCE: 6MILES/9.5KM | TIME: 2.5HOURS | DIFFICULTY: EASY

padstow to constantine bay

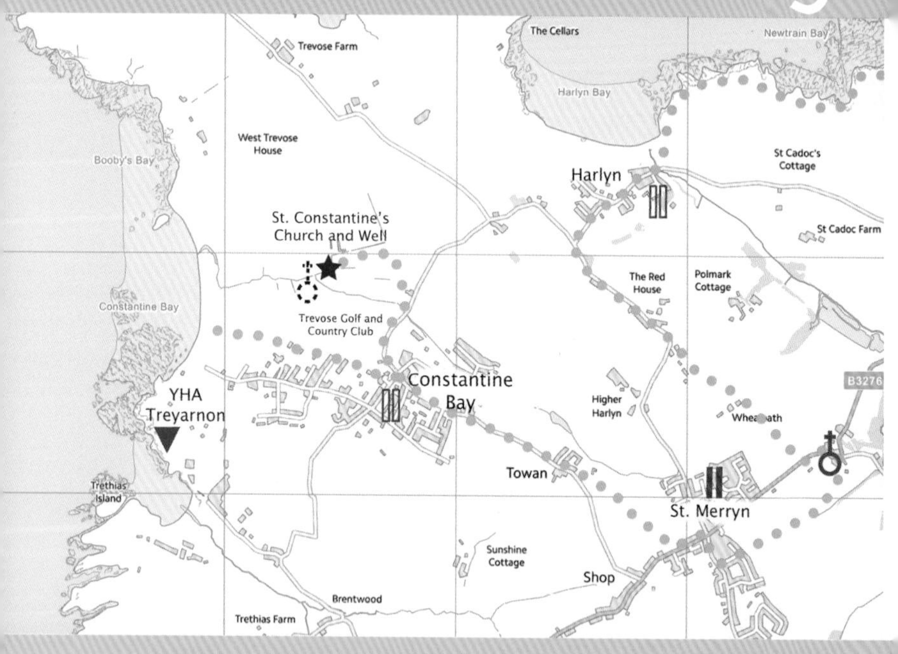

Go out of Padstow churchyard by the main gate and up the hill. Ignore the first right at the side of Prideaux Place Wall. Take the next right, past the entrance keeping Prideaux Place on your right. When the road bends slightly to the right, on the left hand side there is a public footpath/stile through the hedge across two fields to Trethillick Farm (or you can just stay on the road that takes you there anyway!) At the farm lane, turn right and then left onto a lane so that the farm shop entrance is on the left hand side at the crossroads. Continue on the track for about a quarter of a mile. When the track has a fork, take the right hand fork that after a hedge continues on a straight line towards the coast. At the coast, turn left down to Trevone Bay.

Continue on the coast path to the next sandy bay – Harlyn Bay. Leave the coast path at the car park turning right on the road. Stay on the road avoiding the lane on the right hand side to Harlyn. After ¾ mile or so from the car park , the road bends sharply to right. At this point, find the public footpath behind the left hand side house. Take it across the fields towards the church tower. Follow the track that leads to the road opposite the church (to avoid cattle in these fields you may have to continue on road to St. Merryn crossroads and then take left to St. Merryn Church).

After visiting the church, find a stile in the bottom left hand corner of the graveyard, by the grey house, going through the hedge. The footpath runs for several fields, keeping the hedge close by on the left until the stile into bushes at the back of the housing estate on 'Donkey Park'.Take a right at the village road to St. Merryn crossroads. Turn left at the crossroads, past the Farmers Arms on your right. After 30 yards go through the stile in the hedge on the right hand side. Follow the stiles along the fields to a small green at 'Towan'.Turn right onto the road that leads to Constantine Bay. On arriving at the golf course identify the stile at the junction (house and gardens on the left, golf course to the right) that will take you later to Constantine Bay beach. To visit the chapel and well, walk down the narrow road through the golf course. There is a footpath along the hedge. At the T-off for hole 14, there is a way mark post showing 'ahead' and 'left' arrows. Take a left across the grass towards the maintenance works with the hedge on the right hand side. The well is the structure low down with a roof. The chapel is up and inside a small hill beyond it. There is a way mark post beyond the maintenance yard entrance to show you where you can cross the golf course. After visiting, retreat to find the stile to Constantine Bay beach at the junction opposite the club house.

action

Touch the Celtic cross as you leave the door of St. Petroc's Church.

christian reference

Jesus said: 'The kingdom of heaven is like treasure hidden in a field. When a man found it, he hid it again, and then in his joy went and sold all he had and bought that field. Again, the kingdom of heaven is like a merchant looking for fine pearls. When he found one of great value, he went away and sold everything he had and bought it.' *(Matthew 13:44-46)*

harlyn

Harlyn is a place of archaeological finds. In 1900 an Iron Age cemetery was unearthed where there were a hundred slate coffins containing remains and a variety of bronze and iron ornaments. Earlier, in 1864 workmen digging out a pond, found two large beautiful Celtic gold lunulae (named after their crescent, moon-like shape) which are eight inches wide and of fine workmanship, estimated to be from the Beaker period (2,300-2,000 BC). These can be seen in the museum in Truro.

st. merryn church

St. Merryn Churchtown is outside the actual village of St. Merryn. Jeremy Dowling in the *'Church Trails'* card describes St. Merryn Church as 'a sturdy, storm resistant, building'. The original church on the site would have been a rough shelter established about 650. A poem by Shirley Wade can be found on one of the Church walls:

'Memories I hold within my grasp
I'm weakened now, how much longer will I last?
For nearly one thousand years I've

Jesus said: "For where your treasure is, there your heart will be also."

(Matthew 6:21)

stood
A bastion
Another thousand years will pass
Before I crumble and my rubble turn to grass.'

In St. Merryn Church there is an artefact that was discovered in the dunes. It is the font from St. Constantine Chapel, made from cataclews stone from nearby Trevose Head. The font is carved with the twelve apostles depicted around the bowl and is believed to have been made by the craftsman, the Master of St. Endellion. The font contains the inscription, 'May I know your paths and walk in your ways'. The younger (!) Norman font which it replaced is now in Maker Church, near Plymouth. There is also a stone from a Celtic saint's portable altar mounted in the wall above the side chapel altar in St. Merryn Church.

St. Merryn and St. Cadoc

St. Merryn (also known as Marwenna) was one of the major Welsh sixth-century saints and missionary priests. There were a number of religious and educational centres on the south west coast of Wales: Llancafarn was founded and led by St. Cadoc (St. Petroc's nephew) and was where St. Brendan and St. Malo trained. There was also a centre at Llanilltud Fach, which is now known as Llantwit Major led by St. Illtud, and one at Llandough led by St. Drocco.

St. Merryn was a nobleman born in Gwedd or Ceredigion. He studied at Bangor, lived on the Lleyn Peninsula and moved to Brittany where his name is preserved in place names such as Lanmerin, Plomelin, Ploeren, Locmeren des Bois and Locmeren des Pres. St. Merryn is also associated with St. Cadoc, who had established a chapel and holy well close to Harlyn. The source for the well is said to have come from a thirsty St. Cadoc striking the ground with his staff on return from a pilgrimage to St. Michael's Mount with his aunt, St. Keyne, and the water is said to have cured intestinal worms. Only a few fragments remain near St. Cadoc's Farm but there is a restored holy well dedicated to St. Cadoc in the village of St. Mawgan.

Celtic historian, Doble, showed that in the Middle Ages, the name 'St. Merryn' was changed to 'St. Marina' for political reasons, and to undermine the Celtic nature of the church, putting it more under the control of the established Roman Church. The dedication to St. Marina was ratified by Rome in 1338, but St. Marina is an interesting and a less than conventional character: She was a saint from Bithynia who was disguised as a boy in order that she could join a monastery. Her sex was only discovered at her death!

St. Constantine

St. Constantine chapel and well

The Celtic chapel was rebuilt in the fourteenth century but abandoned at the end of the sixteenth century due to encroaching sand and marshland. Of the well it was said that a drought would end if the water was sprinkled on crops. Ray Ramm, in his book on Trevose Golf and Country Club, recounts how Penrose Williams, an amateur archaeologist and doctor, walking near the chapel ruins, sensed the well under his feet in 1908, uncovering it in 1911. This discovery of the well and chapel led to another treasured find for fishermen: the whole area was covered by mussels. The renowned Cornish historian, Charles Henderson, dates this holy well to the third century. The protective roof was built in 1955.

St. Constantine

Were these holy sites dedicated to the Roman Emperor Constantine or to King Constantine of Damnonia (Devon and Cornwall) and cousin of King Arthur or even to a rich man named Constantine who gave up all he owned to become a monk? Certainly the dates of King Constantine of Cornwall, who is said to have been converted to Christianity by St. Petroc in the sixth century, could coincide with the building of the chapel and it is recorded that he gave up his throne at the death of his wife to become a simple monk in Ireland. He was overhead laughing contentedly to himself: 'King Constantine of Cornwall – here I am working in a mill!' The feast day on 9th March is still locally celebrated.

personal reflection

In this part of the walk, I had lots of treasured finds. As I walked across the fields to St. Merryn Church on a stile two scallop shells had been placed, pointing the way to the church. I also met four separate groups of pilgrims and travellers, all with a different attitude to their journey. I was heartened to meet a group setting out on the Saints Way from Padstow full of hope, joy and expectation at what they might discover on their journey together. I met a couple as excited as I was to stumble around the golf course and discover the arch of the overgrown Celtic chapel. I asked a golfer for directions to the chapel who told me that it was a disappointment, as there was nothing to see. I think he just wanted me to get off the golf course! For the golfer, the chapel was an inconvenient ruin in the way, but for me it was the 'treasure hidden in the field', a physical presence that could be seen and touched showing Christians had been here long before.

questions

At Constantine Bay, you will notice grand and often unoccupied properties. Do you think the owners of these large, empty houses have found their treasured place and treasured find?

The former Prime Minister Margaret Thatcher used to holiday in Constantine Bay and she is renowned for her love and pursuit of the economic policy of 'monetarism'. Where does your true treasure lie? In what do you invest your time and resources? Do you invest in material items or does your true treasure lie elsewhere, maybe buried and yet to be discovered?

I have seen the sun break through
to illuminate a small field for
a while, and gone my way and
forgotten it. But that was the pearl
of great price, the one field that had
the treasure in it. I realise now
that I must give all that I have
to possess it. Life is not hurrying
on to a receding future, nor
hankering after an imagined past.
It is the turning aside like Moses
to the miracle of the lit bush, to a
brightness that seemed as transitory
as your youth once, but is the eternity
that awaits you.

R.S.Thomas, The Bright Field

chapter 9
Refuge

constantine bay - st. eval - st. mawgan

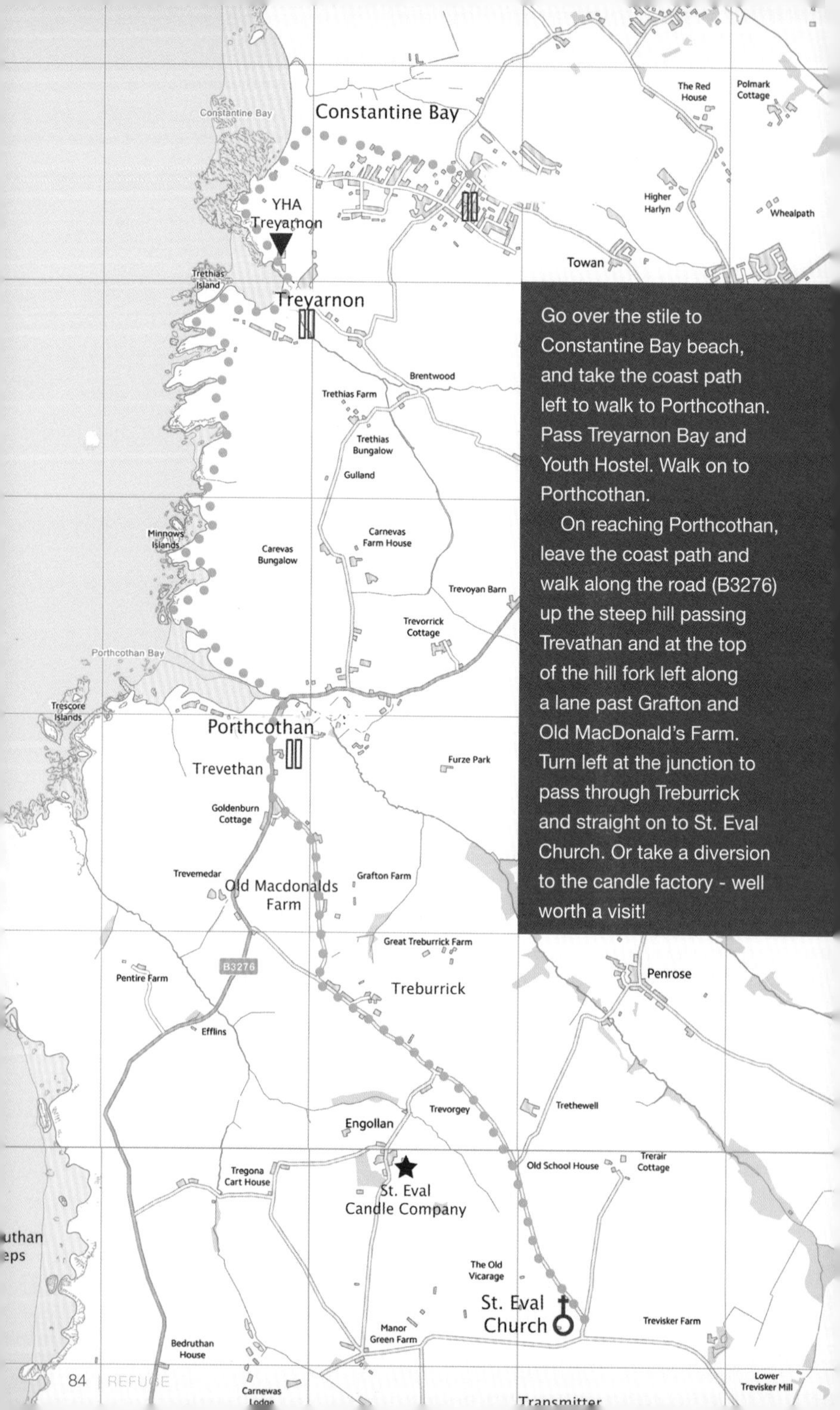

Go over the stile to Constantine Bay beach, and take the coast path left to walk to Porthcothan. Pass Treyarnon Bay and Youth Hostel. Walk on to Porthcothan.

On reaching Porthcothan, leave the coast path and walk along the road (B3276) up the steep hill passing Trevathan and at the top of the hill fork left along a lane past Grafton and Old MacDonald's Farm. Turn left at the junction to pass through Treburrick and straight on to St. Eval Church. Or take a diversion to the candle factory - well worth a visit!

DISTANCE: 5MILES/8KM | TIME: 2.5HOURS | DIFFICULTY: EASY

constantine bay to st. eval

action - beach

Choose a shell from amongst the multi-coloured sand from the beach.

personal reflection

I found the path from the golf course to the beach to be dull, but I was happy to see that someone had put a brightly-coloured windmill on the fence. This made me reflect on how small acts can make a huge difference if walking on a tedious path. However, I then arrived at one of the most beautiful beaches in Cornwall, Constantine Bay, renowned for its surfing but also its coloured sands and millions of shells, like 'a treasure trove'. When I was on the beach, I picked up a dome shaped shell. It reminded me of a tent for shelter, and that led to the theme for this chapter.

For humans and birds, coves, narrow inlets, caves and crevices in the rocks can be sources of refuge and protection from the blasts and stormy seas. Walking this section you will pass Warren Cove, Fox Cove, and others (most are inaccessible from the cliff path). Caves can be secretive, and were involved in smuggling and skulduggery. There is a local story about why the Trevose Head Lighthouse was built in 1847. A brig, *'The Samaritan'* was wrecked off the Bedruthan Steps in 1846, with only two survivors. Locals could soon be seen decked out in finery from the wreckage which they heartlessly called *'The Good Samaritan'* and one of the Bedruthan Steps rocks is now known as 'Samaritan Island'.

At Porthcothan, I tried to take a short cut to Penrose. Fortunately, I met a couple walking their dog who told me that the way via Porthcothan Mill was blocked. I retreated to the café where a

To see a World in a Grain of Sand,
And a Heaven in a Wild Flower,
Hold Infinity in the palm of your hand,
And Eternity in an hour.

William Blake, Extract from Auguries of Innocence, 1803

robin sang around me at the table. The shopkeeper insisted that I visit St. Eval Church and following her advice, I took the road there and found the church to be one of the most evocative, vivid, striking and memorable places on my pilgrimage. Once again, people were put in my path who showed me the best route for the Way.

christian reference

You, you are my refuge and my stronghold,
My God in whom I trust.
(Keith Duke, 'Sacred Weave' 2005)

In God alone is my soul at rest,
he alone is my rock, my strength.
(Margaret Rizza, 2014)

st. eval

Little is known about St. Eval or St. Uvel. The location of St. Eval Church falls between the landing sites of the Welsh and the Irish Celtic missionary expeditions along the coast. St. Eval may have been the Bishop Confessor St. Efelwy/Ufelwy, born in 610 or the son of Ethelbert II born in 749. The church is built on a pre-Christian sacred site: the churchyard and boundary is circular indicating an earlier settlement. A Bronze and Iron Age settlement has been located at Trevisker, one mile to the east of the church, and six sets of barrows were destroyed in the creation of the airfield.

st. eval church

St. Eval Church has stood starkly on the horizon for centuries, battered by wind and rain. It is 100m above sea level, exposed to every Atlantic gale, standing up bravely in the bleak storm-swept landscape. Former vicar of the church, Edward Pruen, said: 'St. Eval has survived the turmoil of history and the relentless Cornish weather' and 'helps us navigate our way though life'. In 1917 Cornish historian, Charles Henderson, dated the tower from 1450 and also wrote: 'St. Eval is one of the roughest and most ungetatable places in the county'. Constructed from 600 tons of local stone from a quarry at Penrose and cataclews from St. Merryn, it has walls five feet thick and the tower is 64 feet high. It was also manned twenty-four hours a day during the Second World War as a look-out post.

Eighteenth century sailors from Bristol returning from voyages on the oceans of the world were heartened by the sight of the church tower that their merchant masters had helped rebuild as an aid to navigation. Seamen's navigation to a safe haven by the stars is also recognised in a window with the inscription: 'The stars will guide you'. The nearby St. Eval RAF base was hastily constructed in 1938-9 and to pilots returning from raids across the Channel, the church became a beacon, a lighthouse, a place of reassurance and refuge. The insignia inscription: 'Faith in our Task', the memorial, cross and window illustrate the recent and ongoing close relationship between the church and the RAF.

questions

Where do you find solace, shelter and protection from the storms of life? Who is your 'very present help' in danger? Where does your true refuge lie? Is it in a building, sturdy or strong? Is it in defence and war? Where is our crag and true haven?

christian reference

Out of the depths I cry to you, Lord.
(Psalm 130:1)

God is our strength and refuge,
Our present help in trouble,
And we therefore will not fear,
Though the earth should change!
Though mountains shake and tremble,
Though swirling floods are raging,
God the Lord of hosts is with us
evermore! (*Words: Richard Bewes, b.1934; Tune: Dambusters March)*

action

Can you find the seven roof bosses that depict *'The Green Man'* who is the guardian of life, fertility symbol and pagan 'spirit of the wild-wood' in both pre-Christian and Christian folklore?

action

Listen to a recording of *'Wild is the wind'* - David Bowie, Nina Simone, Johnny Mathis or others.

DISTANCE: 4MILES/6.5KM | TIME: 1.5HOURS | DIFFICULTY: EASY

St. Eval to St. Mawgan

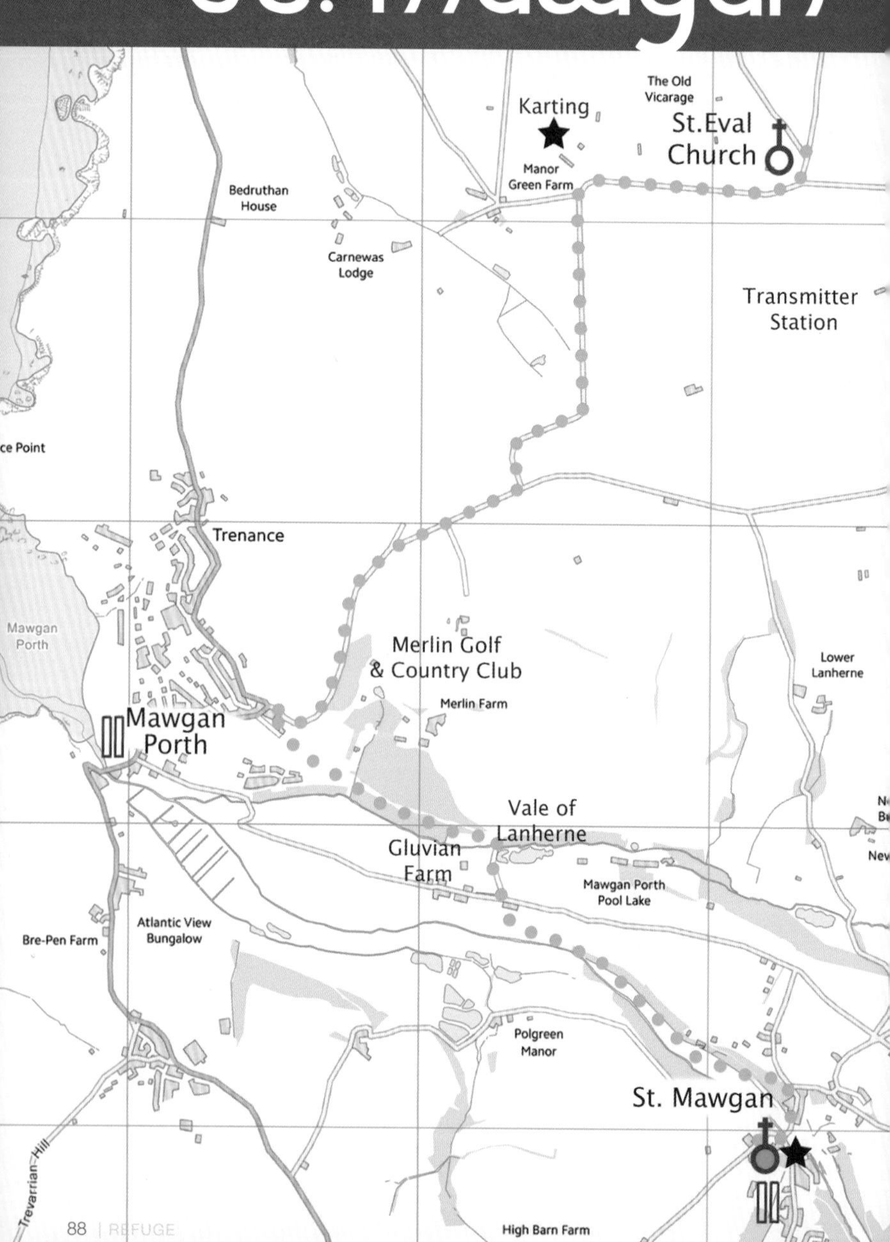

Leave St. Eval Church bearing right around the Transmitter Station to pass 'St. Eval Go Karting Circuit'. After a long trudge, take the road right to Mawgan Porth past the 'Merlin Golf Resort'. You arrive at a corner where the road joins the B3276, turn left. The path now heads back inland. The path is in front of the houses on the left running inland along the valley and gently down. This turns out to be an excellent, straight-forward, well-signposted path in the safety of the woods and ancient pathways of the Vale of Lanherne, a real contrast to the sense of rawness and exposure on the St. Eval plain. At Gluvian Farm camp site, a bridge across the stream leads you to join a lane. Walk up the hill on the lane for a few yards, finding the footpath opposite at the lane junction. Walk on by field and woodland through the valley to the village and on to the beautiful church of St. Mawgan, which with its ancient history, strong Celtic connection and porch shell crosses seems full of life, creativity and vitality.

st. mawgan

St. Mawgan/Maugen/Meugan was a Welsh missionary bishop and an associate of St. Cadoc and St. Breock. St. Mawgan founded a Celtic monastery here, dedicated to St. Herman. The remains of this small, simple structure are in the grounds of nearby Arundell House; a place that continues the Celtic inheritance and maintains monastic life in Cornwall. All three saints (St. Cadoc, St. Mawgan and St. Breock) are associated with East France and Belgium - with place names such as Pleucadeuc, St. Brieuc de Mauron, St. Maugan and Le Meaugon. St. Mawgan may have looked after a monastery in Dementia, now Pembrokeshire.

st. mawgan church

Just inside the lychgate, there is the ancient holy well where St. Mawgan is said to have first preached and baptised. In the churchyard there are crosses: first the Celtic cross by the path, then the Mawgan Celtic cross which was discovered from the aerodrome site in 1942 and is now in 'The Rose Garden', and finally the Medieval lantern cross (similar to the one at St.Wyllow Church, Lanteglos-by-Fowey, and that on St. Michael's Mount).

The churchyard also contains a 'Glastonbury Thorn', which was planted in 1990. It only flowers at Christmas, and is claimed to be a cutting from the true Glastonbury Thorn. This is said to have sprouted from the staff of St. Joseph of Arimathea which he originally grew from the crown of thorns thrust upon Jesus' head at his crucifixion. A 'Glastonbury Thorn' is said to only take root in holy ground.

action

Find the crosses in the churchyard.

st. cadoc

At Ball, once called *'Balleleacadew'*, (which is up the hill from the church and across a field) there is St. Cadoc's well. This marks the place where St. Cadoc, nephew of St. Petroc, built a hermitage so that his friend St. Mawgan could hear his confession.

personal reflection

The Latin root of the words *'navy'* and *'navigation'* is *'navis'*. This root also gives the word *'nave'*, which is thc part of the church where the people sit. The gathered people of the church can be compared to passengers on a ship travelling together towards God. Looking up in the nave, you can see that the barrel-shaped roof of St. Mawgan Church is indeed like the hull of an upturned boat.

song

Calm me Lord, as you calmed the storm,
Still me Lord, keep me from harm,
Let all the tumult within me cease,
Enfold me, Lord, in your peace.
(Margaret Rizza, 1998)

celtic blessing

May God's blessing surround you
and fill your heart,
May Christ walk beside you
And never depart
Holy Spirit keep you faithful and strong to the end
As the stars light your pathway
His love descend.
(St. Mawgan Church Welcome Booklet)

chapter 10

land, air and water

St. Mawgan - Watergate Bay - Newquay

DISTANCE: 2.5MILES/4KM | TIME: 1.5HOURS | DIFFICULTY: EASY

St. Mawgan to Watergate Bay

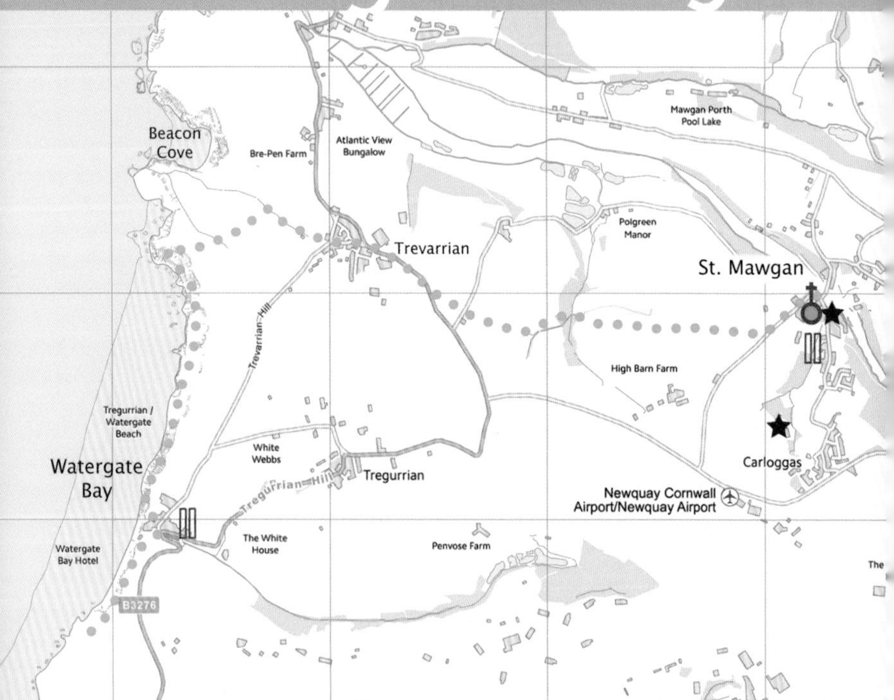

Go up through St. Mawgan churchyard, past the lantern cross and out through a small gate, emerging onto the road. Walk left and aim for the 'No Speed Limit' sign on the right hand side. Just before that you'll see the public footpath sign which leads uphill on a sheltered path, through sheep fields and woodland and over a stream. Eventually you are walking opposite a large pond in a grassy field, go across the stile to your right and then left through a small metal gate. Climb up to the lane, cross, and straight across the next field to the road, walking right to Trevarrian (B3276). At the junction go left, down and into the village of Trevarrian. Then, once you come to another T-Junction, look immediately across the road (and you will see a pathway running along the side of houses). Cross the road and follow the well-defined path to a field gate with a sign 'Watergate Bay 1 mile'. Take this path left, along the upper field boundary and eventually across to the coast path following the National Trust way marker signs. Turn left along the cliff coast path, and on to Watergate Bay.

personal reflection

This section of the Cornish Celtic Way focuses on earth, air and water. Earth: the ancient pathways you walk on from St. Mawgan, imagining the saints and pilgrims of old walking the paths before you, protected by the hedges and maybe carrying goods to or from the sea. Air: as you walk near Newquay Airport where new routes and destinations have been opened up. Water: the surfing sea ahead.

st. columb

Inland from Trevelgue, there is a church dedicated to St. Columb, whose story is about 'flight': St. Columb was a Celtic holy woman who came from Ireland to preach the Gospel in Cornwall and Brittany. Surrounded by a pagan society, St. Columb struggled to maintain her faith and integrity. She was firstly imprisoned by her parents for her faith, 'took flight' from a tyrant who wanted to marry her, was pursued to Cornwall (landing at Trevelgue) but finally beheaded because she refused to renounce her faith or assent to his advances. St. Columb was killed at nearby Ruthvoes, *('ruth' meaning 'red/ blood', 'voes' meaning 'bank')*, from where a spring of water appeared. Traces of the well and chapel can be found.

st. columba

There was another Irish Celtic saint with a similar name, St. Columba *(521-597)*, who also 'took flight' from his home in Ireland to the island of Iona in Scotland because he had caused a tribal dispute that led to a great battle and much killing. St. Columba decided to choose the Celtic course of 'white martyrdom' which means 'exile from his homeland'. Beccan mac Luigdech, an Irish monk writing in 630, said: 'Columba crossed the wave-strewn region, foam-flecked, seal-filled, savage, bounding, seething, white-tipped, doleful' seas. On Iona he founded a missionary base that converted much of Scotland to Christianity. He also inspired St. Aidan to go to Lindisfarne in Northumbria in 635. St. Aidan converted a large portion of the north and the Midlands of England.

personal reflection

'Columb' means *'dove'*, a bird beautiful in flight. Today, so many people are flying from persecution, tyranny, oppression, violence or poverty, and sadly face further suffering or potential death.

questions

As you watch the planes, reflect on the seeming promise of flying to new places and possibilities. What would you be flying away from? What are you expecting to find in your travels? Where are you flying to? What is your destination? St. Columb fought to maintain her beliefs. Do you ever find it difficult to keep your faith going in modern-day society? Have you ever been exposed to new opportunities through 'taking flight' from your home?

You have searched me Lord,
and you know me.
You know when I sit and when I rise;
You perceive my thoughts from afar.
You discern my going out
and my lying down;
You are familiar with all my ways.

If I rise on the wings of the dawn,
if I settle on the far side of the sea,
Even there your hand will guide me,
Your right hand will hold me fast.

(Psalm 139:1-3, 9-10)

DISTANCE: 3.5MILES/5KM | TIME: 1.5HOURS | DIFFICULTY: EASY

Watergate Bay to Newquay

Follow the coast path from Watergate Bay to Porth. Crossing the bridge and onto the fine sandy beach and then on in to Newquay, passing Lusty Glaze and Tolcarne beaches. Continue walking into Newquay town centre.

watergate bay

At Watergate Bay you will see the increasing influence of surf and food culture. As well as being famous for pasties, Cornwall is becoming a 'foodie' destination, with renowed local chefs such as Nathan Outlaw and Ben Tunnicliffe. At Watergate Bay, there is Jamie Oliver's 'Fifteen' restaurant.

newquay

Newquay and the surrounding area has been well known since surfing took off to the UK in the 1960s. It is home to the World Surf League qualifying competition and the music festival 'Boardmasters'. Many people take flight and move down to Newquay with an idealistic picture of the surfing lifestyle.

water

The Celts believed in the power of water. They regarded streams and rivers as sacred and water rising out of a rock as miraculous. Often they worshipped, Christianised and built holy wells around these water sources. Wells were places of gathering, places to hear the village gossip and where passing saints might preach. Celts believed that wells had special healing powers and believed in immersing themselves in the healing power of water to gain a cure.

personal reflection

I'm not a surfer myself, but love swimming in the sea and I know the exhilaration you can gain whilst body-boarding as the waves crash upon you. Immersing yourself completely in the water can be a very therapeutic, cathartic and cleansing experience. There are charities which use surfing as therapy and rehabilitation.

Surfers have to engage with the elements and learn to work with the swell, wind and tides. Just as farmers know the coming changeability of the weather, so surfers have a keen knowledge of the conditions - whether the surf is 'messy' or 'clean' and how to use the sea's power to their advantage. Writing about the experience of surfing,

Duke Boyd talked about 'the man upon the board shutting out the world and its clamour for the silence of the rolling green passageways of bliss and beauty', and about surfing being 'a trip through the sunshines of time and eternity with bare feet and blue soul'. Thomas Mitchell said that 'the soul surfer expresses himself through the unity of the breaking wave. He borrows the wave's spirit for a while and uses his body and equipment to translate the essence of the wave's spirit into art.... he becomes one with the wave, his body and his board are extensions of his mind.' I would not want to claim anything specifically 'Christian' about surfing, but there is a spiritual aspect in a surfer's engagement with the water. Watching or taking part in surfing can be part of your spiritual journey, and can be an expression of spirituality in the 21st Century. Writers Ford and Brown claim it is a reinterpretation of the values of spirituality aesthetics and the quest for inner peace and authenticity. Surfing can lead to a real respect for nature and the environment, and this care for creation is expressed by beach cleans organised by Surfers Against Sewage and others.

Perhaps surfers can inspire our spirituality by their persistence and their passion for the perfect wave. Perhaps they can inspire us to invigorate a tired, washed-up church. I laughed when I saw a café in Newquay named 'The Beached Lamb'- this to me was a metaphor for a church in need of help to get back in the water!

questions

Watch the surfers in the sea. How can you become more patient and determined in your life? How can you work with and respect the elements? In what ways can you invigorate your own spirituality?

surfer's prayer

O God of surfing, wind and sea
Let thy bounty come to me.
Give me large, give me small,
Any size, I'd take them all.
Just to rise upon the face,
To see the crest, my heart will race.
I feel the sea within my veins
But I know it's you who holds the reins.
If I fall then drop me slow,
As wipeouts come and wipeouts go
I give my life without a fee
This I pray, my God of sea.
(Doug Rhodes, Surfers' Prayer, from the Annapolis Surf Club)

Always looking for calm water -
but calm may only be found in a pond.
The unbounded ocean
is where I must
become at home
with its
breaks and troughs
with its
rips and sheens
with its
storms and wells.

Ian Adams, The Unbounded Ocean, from Unfurling, 2014

chapter 11

secrets uncovered

newquay - crantock - holywell -cubert - st. piran's oratory

DISTANCE: 3.5MILES/5.5KM | TIME: 2HOURS | DIFFICULTY: EASY

Newquay to Crantock

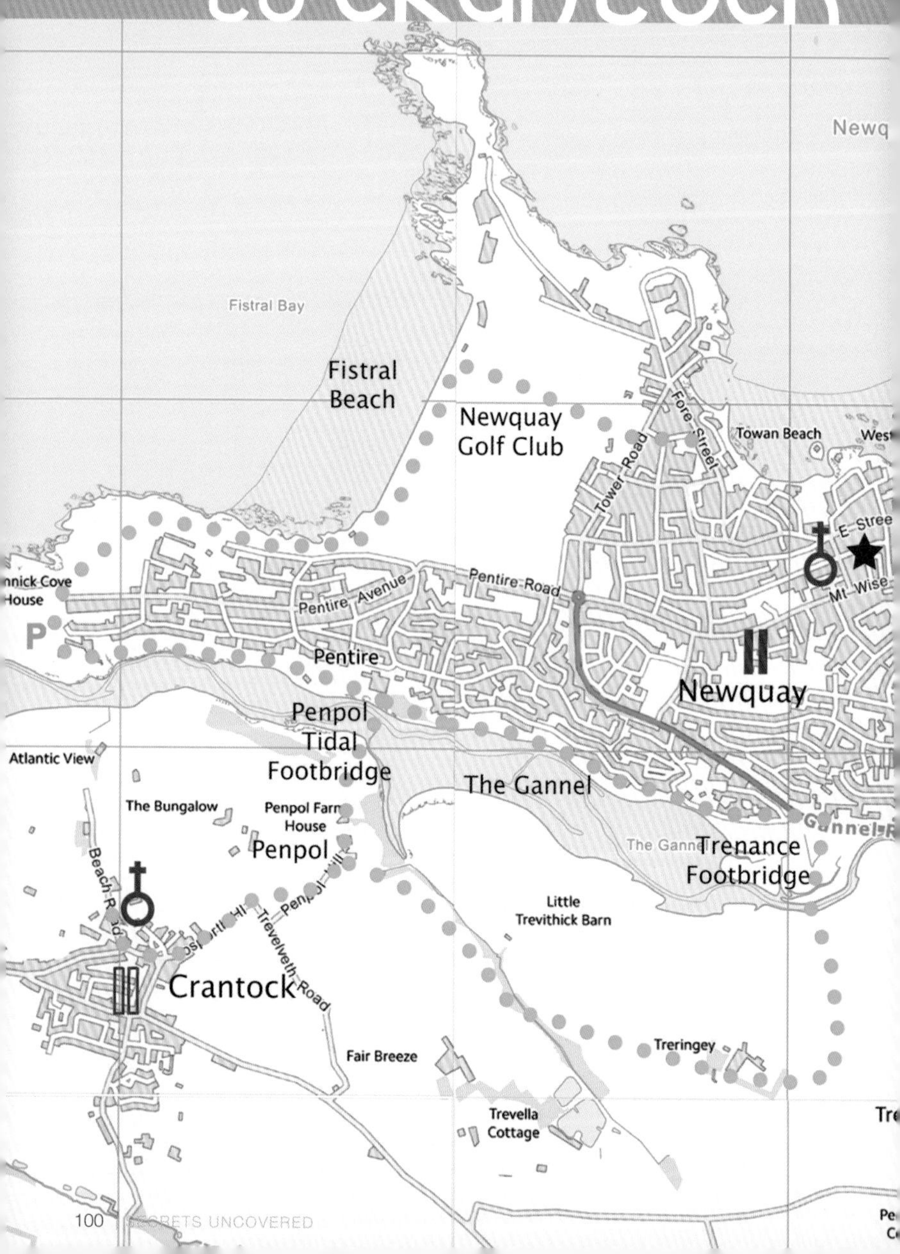

Walk downhill through Newquay town centre to North Quay Hill, come to the roundabout with 'The Red Lion' pub in one corner, go up the hill to 'Toby Lane' and just before what looks like an old chapel you come to a path that leads you through the golf course to Fistral Beach. At Fistral Beach follow the golf course fence, keeping the golf course on your left hand side, the beach dunes on the right until you reach the south end of Fistral Beach. Follow the coast path to the headland.

Pentire Point is one of the oldest places of settlement in Cornwall, an iron age ring. At the car park on Pentire Point, find the road 'Riverside Avenue' behind and among the houses. To get to Crantock, you need to cross the River Gannel. For the summer ferry go down by the 'Fern Pit Café' or continue walking half a mile down until the path drops down to the river (The first signpost may lead you to a riverside path which is impassable at high tide). The second path drops down to a wooden bridge marked by a yellow and red sign. This is the Penpol tidal footbridge. (If this is impassable you will have to walk further inland to the Trenance footbridge.) Cross and go straight up a small river valley opposite the Penpol tidal footbridge, then get on a bridge going up a lane to the right.

Continue on the road bearing left at the top of the hill to the village of Crantock (you can avoid two sides of a field on the road, by following a footpath right across the field). In Crantock find the church.

notes on this section:

Before setting out, look at the tide times so that you can cross the Gannel River. In high season, there are two boat ferry points that can carry you across the estuary, or you may be able to cross the water, as we were fortunate enough to be able to do, by the Penpol tidal footbridge. This is submerged and hidden except for two markers; and is only revealed for a couple of hours either side of low tide. At all times you can follow the coast path inland and around by the Trenance footbridge.

song

Wade in the water
Wade in the water, children,
Wade in the water
God's a-going to trouble the water

Look over yonder, what do you see?
God's a-going to trouble the water
The Holy Ghost a-coming on me
God's a-going to trouble the water
(*Traditional spiritual song*)

St Carantoc

There are twelfth century Latin records of St. Carantoc's life in a library in Wales. St. Carantoc was the son of Ceredig, a minor Welsh chieftain, who gave his name to 'Ceredigion'. St. Carantoc gave up his right to the throne to learn the religious life in Ireland under St. Patrick, his tutor and friend. Starting off from Ireland in a coracle, St. Carantoc cast his small altar stone into the sea as a guide (there was one of these stones set in the wall in St. Merryn Church). St. Carantoc was accompanied by his pet dove.

On arrival in Cornwall, coming ashore on the bank of the River Gannel, St. Carantoc wanted to build his church close by the water's edge, but his dove took the shavings that he had produced for lighting a fire and carried them to the current site of Crantock Church. St. Carantoc saw this a sign of guidance from the Holy Spirit (the Gospels describe the Holy Spirit as wind, breath, fire and a dove). St. Carantoc is depicted in the Penkridge-stone statue located in Crantock Church, with a book and spade (suggesting work by the hand and brain) and with a dove on his arm. To this day, doves still live in Crantock.

St. Carantoc made Crantock a missionary centre, and was the leader of a group that included St. Enodoc and St. Columb. Like St. Petroc, St. Carantoc showed an affinity for animals: King Arthur asked St. Carantoc to rid the land of a marauding dragon: 'Then the blessed Carantoc prayed to the Lord and immediately the dragon came running to him, making a loud noise and it humbly bent its head before the servant of God, who puts his stole (a priest's scarf) around its neck and led it like a lamb, not lifting its wings or claws'. St. Carantoc did not kill the dragon but sent it away without harm.

action

Whilst I was in Crantock Church an Australian was visiting to see the handiwork carved by his female ancestor. He pointed out the dove with the wood shaving in its beak in the vicar's stall. In Crantock Church, you can admire many beautiful carvings. Can you find the beautiful dove?

personal reflection

The dove revealed to St. Carantoc the place he should build his church. This day, for me, was all about waiting, pausing, giving time and being patient and then being given the grace to see hidden things being revealed. When we arrived at The River Gannel we couldn't see anywhere to cross, we just had to sit and wait for half an hour and trust the advice of the walkers: that a way across the water would be revealed. As the tide receded, the water rippled and the slatted path formed in front of us.

christian reference

Jesus said: 'For there is nothing hidden that will not be disclosed, and nothing concealed that will not be known or brought out into the open.' *(Luke 8:17)*

DISTANCE: 2MILES/3KM | TIME: 1HOUR | DIFFICULTY: EASY

Crantock to Holywell

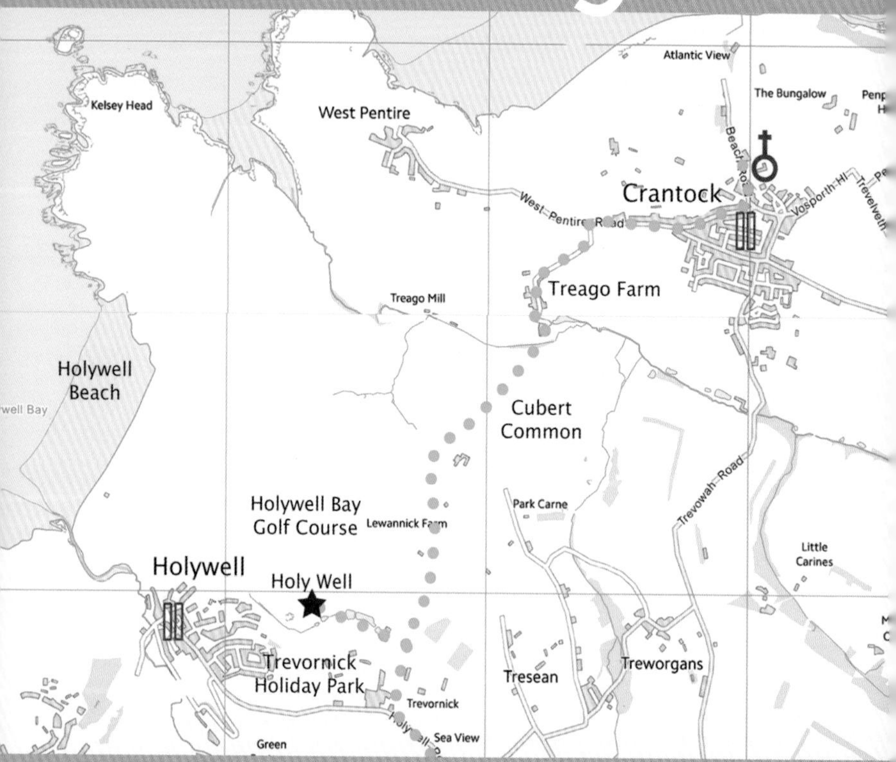

Leave the village green in Crantock, passing the Post Office/shop on your left. At the junction turn right towards West Pentire. Just after leaving Crantock village, take a left down the farm lane towards Treago Farm, past farm buildings, following the lane into a valley. Then follow footpath signs across common land to Holywell following the post markers up the hill. You gain an expansive vista crossing Cubert Common, and Porth Joke and Holywell Bay are particularly stunning areas of coastline. Keep straight ahead at the first footpath junction. Pass the five bar gate on your left and then bear immediately left with the field boundary on your left. Bear right at the next junction towards Holywell, follow the path along the golf-club boundary. At the golf club find the Holy Well: take a right along by the fish ponds, find a white path at the top of a hill near a hut and trees. At this point bear left to the T-off for the 17th hole to find steps down to the Holy Well.

personal reflection

If I was discouraged by a golfer at Constantine Bay, I was then rewarded by my encounter with the Trevornick holiday club bears training for the summer season. My guide was not a dove, but 6'5" children's holiday club camp site bears! They suddenly appeared in our path when we were searching for the holy well and guided us to the fish ponds and the well.

The well was gushing with water, and is believed to have had healing properties. It was a treasured find and shown to me by the most unlikely and surprising of way markers and guides. There is another holy well in a cave accessible at low tide at Holywell Bay.

christian reference

Jesus said 'If you knew the gift of God and who it is that asks you for a drink, you would have asked him and he would have given you living water.' 'Sir,' the woman said 'you have nothing to draw with, and the well is deep. Where can you get this life-giving water?'

Jesus answered 'Everyone who drinks this water will be thirsty again, but whoever drinks the water I give them will never thirst. Indeed, the water that I give them will become in them a spring of water welling up to eternal life'. *(John 4:10-11, 13-14).*

Come to the well and meet your Saviour
Offering water of life
Come to the well if you are thirsty
Drink of the water of life

Refresh your spirit
Revive your soul
Ease your troubled mind

Quench your thirst
Lighten your burdens
Be born again today

Be washed through
And made anew
Be filled with hope and love

Annie HenryHolland, Come to the Well, 2017

directions

Leave Holywell Bay Golf Club. At the road, turn left along the pavement by the road to Cubert village. Note: St. Cubert's Church spire could inspire and spur you on your way!

Go to the back of Cubert Church graveyard, through the houses to find a footpath stile into a field. Follow the boundary to the right and down, coming upon Trebisken House. Turn right on the farm lane, then at the footpath junction turn left, through the gate and down a path by a hedgerow and under trees. This comes out at a bridge. Follow the path through a wood and marsh, over grassland to a lane. Turn right up the steep hill for nearly a mile to Gear Farm. After this take the right-hand footpath to St. Piran's Church and Oratory. The church is to be found after ¾ mile(1km) by following the white stones and black acorn footpath markers. The oratory is to west of the church.

We found both difficult to find. If you lose your way, go to the modern cross erected in 1969 high up on the dunes. You can look down from that higher point to locate both the oratory and church.

DISTANCE: 4MILES/6.5KM | TIME: 1.75HOURS | DIFFICULTY: EASY

holywell to St. Piran's Oratory

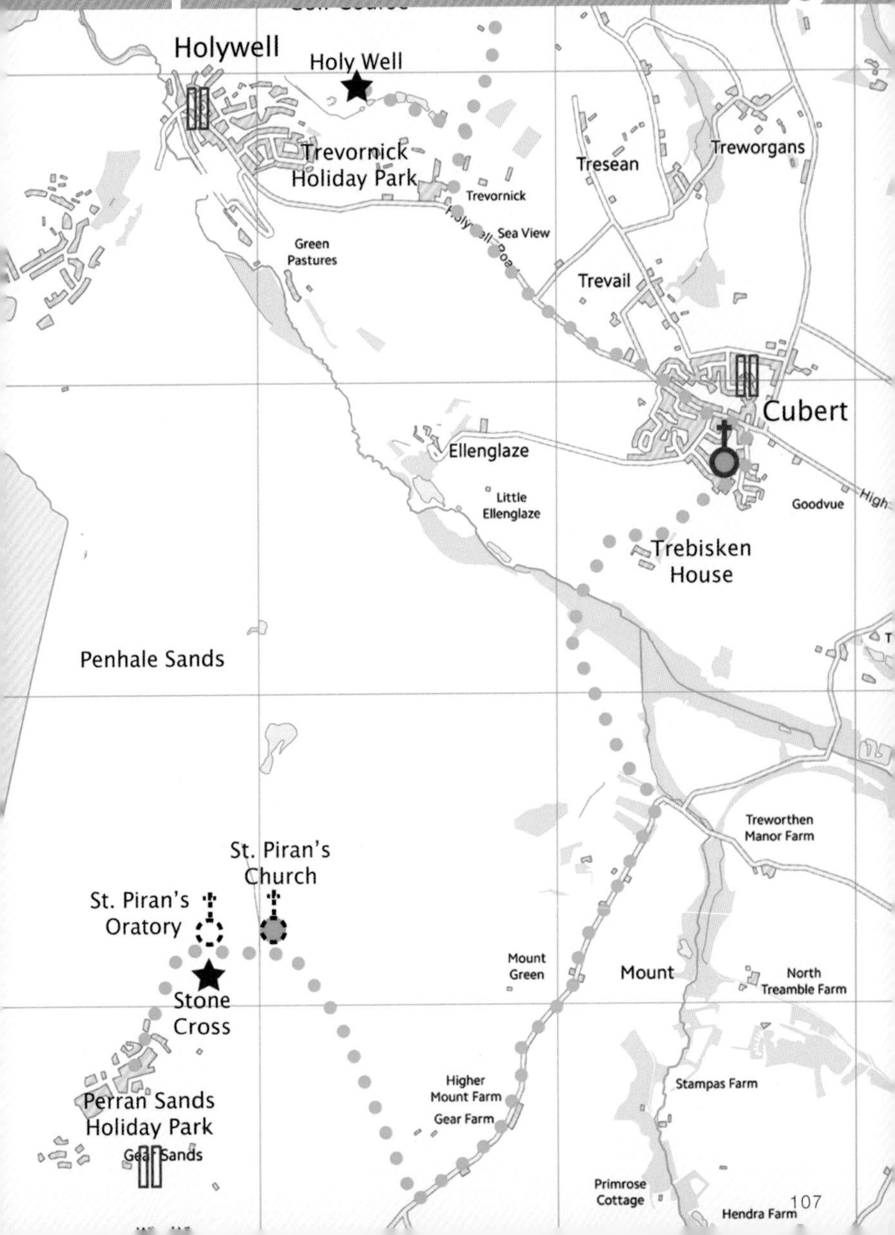

St. Cubert

St. Cubert is probably St. Gwbert of Cardigan in West Wales. Little else is known about him except that he was part of the missionary endeavour led by St. Carantoc. The historian, Orme, argued that St. Cubert's name is a derivation of St. Cuthbert *(634-687)* of Lindisfarne in Northumbria, but others agree with the historian, Doble, that St. Gwbert of Wales is the much more likely contender.

Action

In Cubert Church look for the seventh century pillar built into the west wall of the tower and touch the seventh century cross at the north door.

St. Piran's Oratory

Many have stumbled across these sands before you: together with St. Michael's Mount and Holy Trinity Chapel at St. Day, St. Piran's Oratory was one of the three great places of Cornish pilgrimage in Medieval times. St. Piran's name is venerated nearby in many places, such as Perranwell, Perranarworthal, Perranuthnoe and in Cardiff and in Brittany too.

The oratory housed St. Piran's relics. (An oratory, in early times, was a chapel built over a tomb). St. Piran's head is believed to have been discovered in the sands in the twentieth century, but was then lost or stolen. St. Piran came from Ireland and was said to have been tossed over a cliff by a jealous Irish king afraid of Piran or 'Ciaran's' healing powers. With a millstone around his neck, (this could have been a portable altar like that of St. Carantoc or a 'killick' stone still used as an anchor in small boats by Cornish fishermen), the storm immediately abated and St. Piran was carried to Cornwall, landing at Perran Sands. St. Piran established his cell, church and community. The remaining oratory is one of the oldest Celtic chapels in Cornwall and Britain, *'Perranzabuloe'* meaning *'Perran in the sands'*.

This is a story of covering and being uncovered: through the centuries there has been a struggle against encroaching sands (and vandalism too) and the oratory was only revealed again by shifting sands in 1800 and then was covered up for a while. A bunker was built around the oratory but the site still is sometimes waterlogged. On St. Piran's feast day, 5th March, people stream across the dunes to re-enact the story of St. Piran's life. Grants are currently being sought to permanently cover, drain and restore the oratory.

Echoing the affinity of St. Petroc and St. Carantoc with animals, St. Piran's first converts were said to have been a fox, badger and a boar (other stories also include a wolf and a doe). St. Piran is also said to have encouraged tin mining, seeing white tin stream out of a black ore rock and hence the colours on the Cornish flag, St. Piran's Cross, and his patronage of tin miners. St. Piran is believed to have often got drunk, hence the Cornish saying 'as drunk as a Perraner' and he lived to a great age.

action

The original church and cell were abandoned in the eleventh century and replaced by a church of Norman origin in 1150, built on higher ground. Here you will also find a Celtic cross of ninth century origin which you can touch.

christian reference

Almighty God,
You sent your servant St. Piran
across the stormy seas
to bring your Word, your Light and
your Healing
to the people of Cornwall
May we too be like St Piran:
never letting the fire of your Spirit
be quenched within us.
Like tin rising out of the rock
make us wellsprings of eternal life
in service of your Son our Saviour Jesus
Christ our Lord.
Amen.

St. Piran came across the sea,
to teach the Cornish how to be.
He longed to share his Saviour's love,
tell of God's grace from up above.

St. Piran, St. Piran,
friend of animals and men,
St. Piran, St. Piran,
tell your story again.

St. Piran landed on the sand,
gave God thanks to be on land,
but no man would come around
only four legged friends did abound.

Legend has it a wild boar
a badger and a fox came forth,
They sensed St. Piran's childlike love,
closer to his camp they moved.

He shared his water and his food,
soon there was a happy mood,
The Cornish wondered at this sight,
welcomed him with songs so bright.

St. Piran told the Bible tales,
round the fire they listened well,
then from the flames white ore appeared,
St. Piran had discovered tin.

(Annie Henry Holland, St Piran's Song, 2011)

chapter 12

good samaritans

st. piran's oratory - perranporth - st. agnes - porthtowan

DISTANCE: 5.8MILES/9KM | TIME: 2.5HOURS | DIFFICULTY: CHALLENGING

ST. PIRAN'S ORATORY TO ST. AGNES

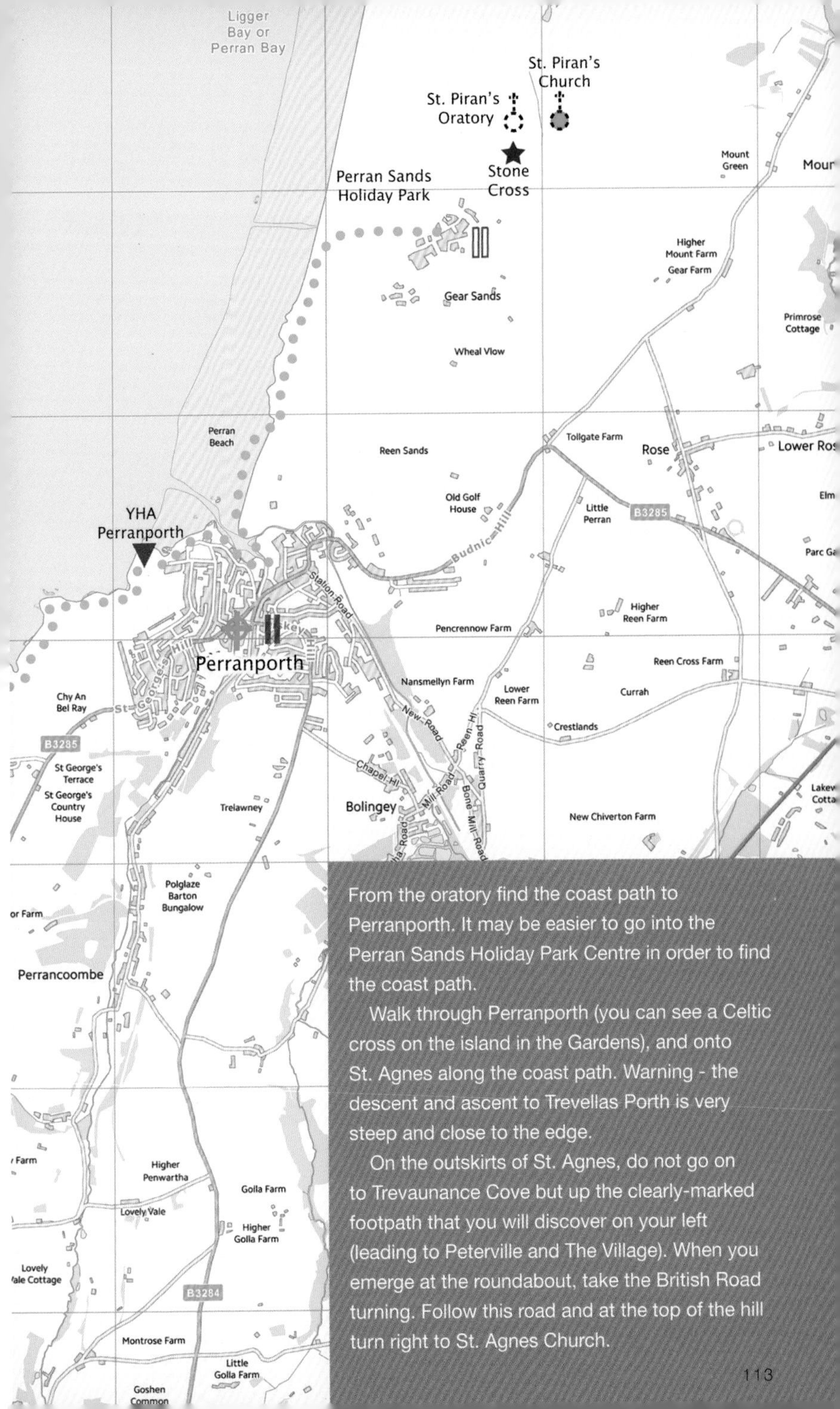

From the oratory find the coast path to Perranporth. It may be easier to go into the Perran Sands Holiday Park Centre in order to find the coast path.

Walk through Perranporth (you can see a Celtic cross on the island in the Gardens), and onto St. Agnes along the coast path. Warning - the descent and ascent to Trevellas Porth is very steep and close to the edge.

On the outskirts of St. Agnes, do not go on to Trevaunance Cove but up the clearly-marked footpath that you will discover on your left (leading to Peterville and The Village). When you emerge at the roundabout, take the British Road turning. Follow this road and at the top of the hill turn right to St. Agnes Church.

St. Agnes

mining industry

There is evidence of the flourishing of copper and tin mining in this area with many abandoned mine-shafts and engine houses on the path. For example, at Polberro, near St. Agnes, 450 people were employed in the tin and copper mining workings in 1838. On the path from St. Agnes to Porthtowan there is the dramatic old engine house of Wheal Coates (the pumping and winding houses are from 1872, the engine house from 1880 and the calciner from 1913). Some of the mines only had a few years' life in the second half of the nineteenth century and at Trevellas Porth on the way to St. Agnes there is a sign to 'Blue Hills Mining', the only tin mine still active in Cornwall. St. Agnes previously had an active harbour, with a thriving pilchard fishing industry.

action

The coast path immerses us in the industrial tin and copper mining heritage of Cornwall. No longer driven forward by church towers on the horizon, our view is drawn to the next mining stack. Although we might be fascinated by Cornwall's industrial past, we can also be encouraged by contributions to the many cairns along the path today, and by the Celtic cross on the island in Perranporth Gardens. You can touch the cross outside St. Agnes Church (which I found very helpful after the long haul along the coast path). I failed to find the place of St. Agnes' well on the way down to Chapel Porth Beach and here our Celtic trail fades and goes a little cold.

questions

Each generation leaves its mark and then is superseded by another. What is important or of value to you? What period of history is important to you?

christian reference

Jesus said: 'A man was going down from Jerusalem to Jericho, when he was attacked by robbers. They stripped him of his clothes, beat him and went away, leaving him half-dead. A priest happened to be going down the same road, and when he saw the man, he passed by on the other side. So too, a Levite, when he came to the place and saw him, passed by on the other side. But a Samaritan, as he travelled came where the man was; and when he saw him, he took pity on him. He went to him and bandaged his wounds, pouring on oil and wine. Then he put the man on his own donkey, brought him to an inn, and he took care of him. The next day he took out two denarii (two days' wages) and gave them to the innkeeper. 'Look after him,' he said, 'and when I return, I will reimburse you for any extra expense you may have'. Jesus said 'Which of these three was a neighbour to the man who fell into the hands of robbers?' The expert in the law replied, 'The one who had mercy on him'. Jesus told him, 'Go and do likewise'. *(Luke 10:30-37)*

personal reflection

Throughout the entire stretch of the walk, I was followed by a helicopter patrolling the coastline. As I climbed through this post-industrial landscape of mine-workings and quarries on the path from Perranporth to St. Agnes, with many places and rocks for any potential robbers or muggers to hide behind, the story (or parable) Jesus told of *'The Good Samaritan'* strongly came to mind. The road from Jerusalem to Jericho is steep, barren and lonely. On this lonely part of the path, I thought about and gave thanks for the many people along the coastline who look out for us: the Coastwatch volunteers, the Coastguard and the RNLI, keeping the beaches, sea and cliffs safe for all and rescuing and caring for people when they get into trouble. These are the 'Good Samaritans' of the shoreline. Jesus' story speaks to the British psyche of helping people regardless of their situation, racial identity, religious affiliation or ability to pay, an ethos that the creation of the National Health Service embodies. The NHS is a practical outworking and expression of this story, which I believe is our national parable: it is the story of Jesus that people today most readily recognise and use to inform their daily actions.

st. agnes

St. Agnes gives her name to the village and church of this coastline, St Agnes Head and Beacon, and the well and oratory at Chapel Porth, as well as to one of the Isles of Scilly.

St. Agnes was a Roman martyr who died in the early fourth century. She may never have come to Cornwall, particularly as she is reportedly killed in her teenage years, yet local legend has it that she did, escaping from prison in Rome and voyaging to Cornwall. She is said to have landed at Perranarworthal, established a base by the coast line at Chapel Porth and at St. Agnes, where many miraculous tales are told of her turning the devil to stone and defeating the giant Bolster, by tumbling him over a cliff. The rocks around St. Agnes represent the giant she overthrew.

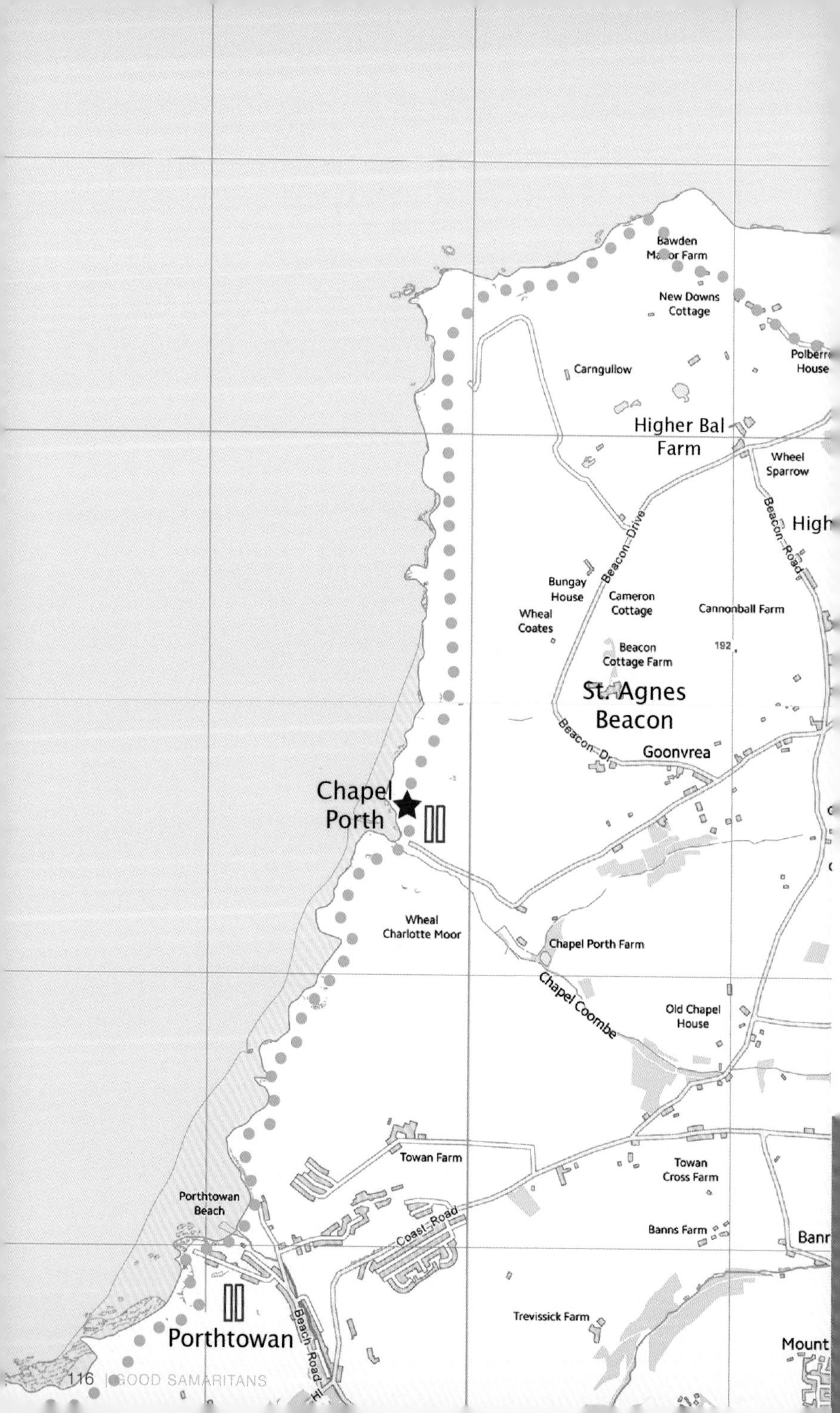

Bawden
Manor Farm
New Downs
Cottage
Carngullow
Polberro
House
Higher Bal
Farm
Wheel
Sparrow
Beacon Drive
Beacon Road
High
Bungay
House
Cameron
Cottage
Cannonball Farm
Wheal
Coates
Beacon
Cottage Farm
192
St. Agnes
Beacon
Beacon Dr
Goonvrea
Chapel
Porth
Wheal
Charlotte Moor
Chapel Porth Farm
Chapel Coombe
Old Chapel
House
Towan Farm
Towan
Cross Farm
Porthtowan
Beach
Coast Road
Banns Farm
Trevissick Farm
Porthtowan
Beach Road
Mount

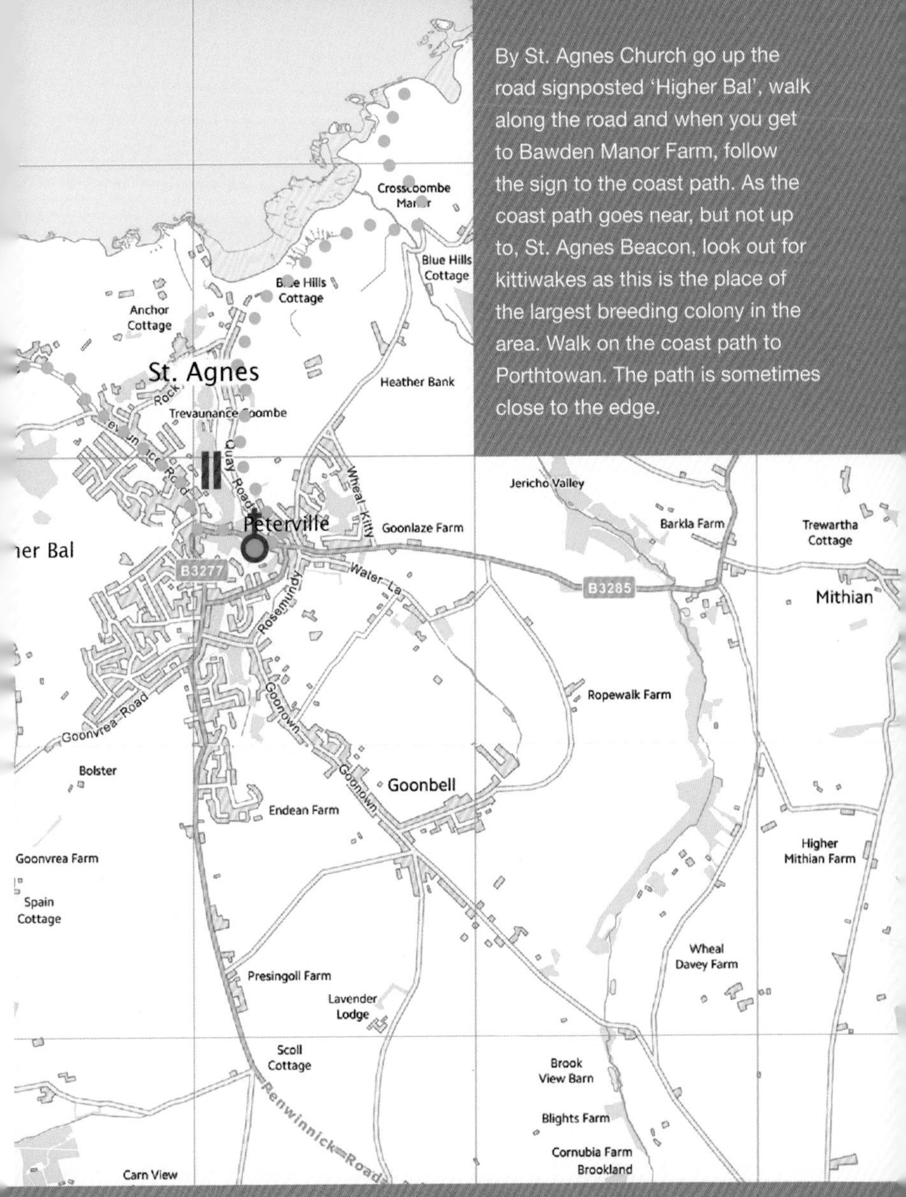

By St. Agnes Church go up the road signposted 'Higher Bal', walk along the road and when you get to Bawden Manor Farm, follow the sign to the coast path. As the coast path goes near, but not up to, St. Agnes Beacon, look out for kittiwakes as this is the place of the largest breeding colony in the area. Walk on the coast path to Porthtowan. The path is sometimes close to the edge.

DISTANCE: 4MILES/6.5KM | TIME: 2HOURS | DIFFICULTY: CHALLENGING

St. Agnes to Porthtowan

personal reflection

Much of this walk is along the coast path with some stunning scenery, perilous drops and long, fine sandy beaches. However, after the rich aspect of the Celtic quest, and the discoveries and encounters of the saints, I found this part of the route quite a slog along lonely paths. Sometimes, when life is bleak and the road ahead obscured and clouded, you can lose your perspective, your heart and your focus; then I find it important to draw on other sources for inspiration: novels, music, theatre and art. Being around artists I find is particularly helpful. West Cornwall is a place of many artists and people of vision, who help us see in new ways and offer new perspectives. William Blake wrote 'learning how to see is the beginning of wonder'. No great Cornish art survives from the Celtic period, such as we find in other Celtic lands of the same time: the beautifully and intricately drawn illuminated manuscripts such as you can find in *'The Book of Kells'* or *'The Lindisfarne Gospels'*, written around 668, or the extremely fine and intricate filigree and craftsmanship found in the recently discovered Staffordshire Hoard. Celtic monasteries were not permanent, but merely a collection of temporary wattle and daub huts on a stone base grouped together around a central tree or church, such as you can find in Skellig Michael in Northern Ireland. The great contemporary Celtic saint and founder of the monastery on Iona in Scotland, St. Columba, described them as 'colonies of heaven' where there was hospitality, solace, healing, prayer, study and art all being accomplished in the heart of the so-called Dark Ages. Ian Bradley described them as 'a combination of commune; retreat house; seats of education and learning; mission station; hotel; school; hospital; university; arts centre encouraging knot-work, clothing, pottery, metalwork and woodwork and a powerhouse for the community: a source of spiritual energy, hospitality, learning and cultural enlightenment.' They were stopping-off points, places of respite, for a people on the move, in a state of transition. The church in our time can at best be this too, providing enlightenment and light, culture and learning, peace and hospitality in a dark and difficult world. When we become lost or jaded, artists, poets and dreamers are those who can point us towards a better future.

St. Agnes, in her short life, was pursued by many suitors in Rome, but nonetheless kept faithful only to Christ, saying: 'Jesus Christ is my only spouse'; and her single-minded devotion, dedication and determination could be of help and solace to us when we feel like we are losing our way or our faith.

chapter 13

to the lighthouse or into hell's mouth

porthtowan - portreath - gwithian

DISTANCE: 4MILES/6.5KM | TIME: 1.5HOURS | DIFFICULTY: CHALLENGING

Porthtowan to Portreath

Follow the coast path which is sometimes close to the edge.

Portreath

Christian Reference

May God shield us by each sheer drop,
May Christ keep us in each rock-path
May the Spirit fill us on each bare slope
As we cross hill and plain. Amen.

Jesus said: 'Come to me, all who are weary and burdened, and I will give you rest.' *(Matthew 11:28)*

Personal Reflection

This is a particularly gruelling part of the walk. Although it is very beautiful, with bright turquoise seas and precipitous cliff drops, we continue to travel through a post-industrial, worn and battered landscape. Four times you have to descend sharply into a valley and ascend just as sharply on the other side. It is an exhausting process and hard work. Hard times in a spiritual journey are important.

I am interested that Jesus throughout his life withdraws to lonely places to pray *(Mark 1:35, Mark 6:30-32, Luke 5:16, Luke 6:12)* and to be strengthened, and when Jesus was in the wilderness, angels ministered to him. The Desert Fathers and the Celtic saints set up their cells on exposed, weather-beaten and lonely outcrops in order to pray, overcome the world and draw on the love of God.

Questions

What have you had to confront and face up to about yourself or your situation on this journey? What burdens have you had lifted?

Personal Reflection

Portreath arose out of the copper mining boom, and claimed to be the copper capital of the world in the nineteenth century serving the mining area of nearby and larger Redruth. (Although I did feel that the Portreath history board was stretching it a bit, claiming the local mining heritage to be the 'Eighth Wonder of the World'!)

The soul comes to a valley. For in the valleys and the low places, the struggles against the devil and opposing powers take place. In the valley, the battle must be fought. Therefore this wanderer of ours descends to those in the deep and low places, not to linger there, but to gain victory there.

(Early Christian writer, Origen)

DISTANCE: 7.75MILES/12.5KM | TIME: 3HOURS | DIFFICULTY: CHALLENGING

portreath to gwithian

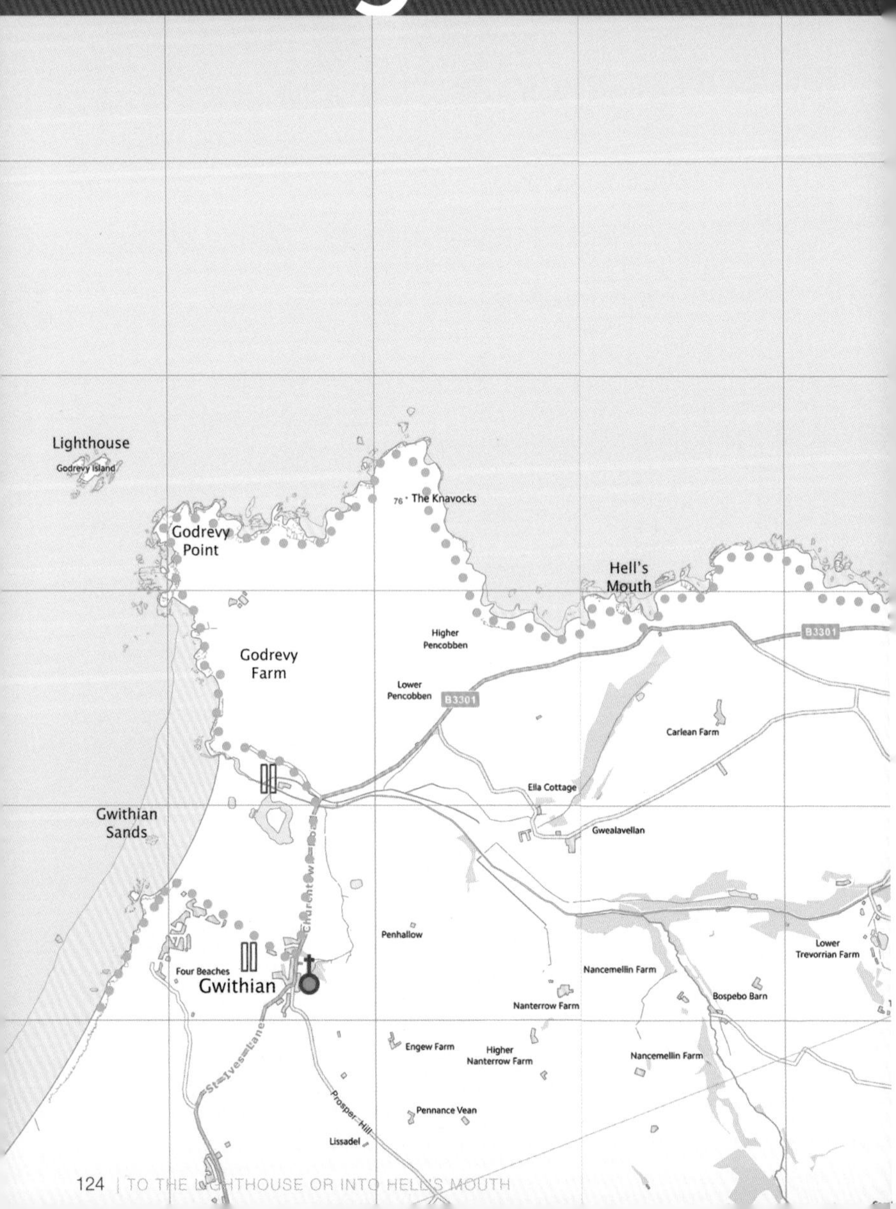

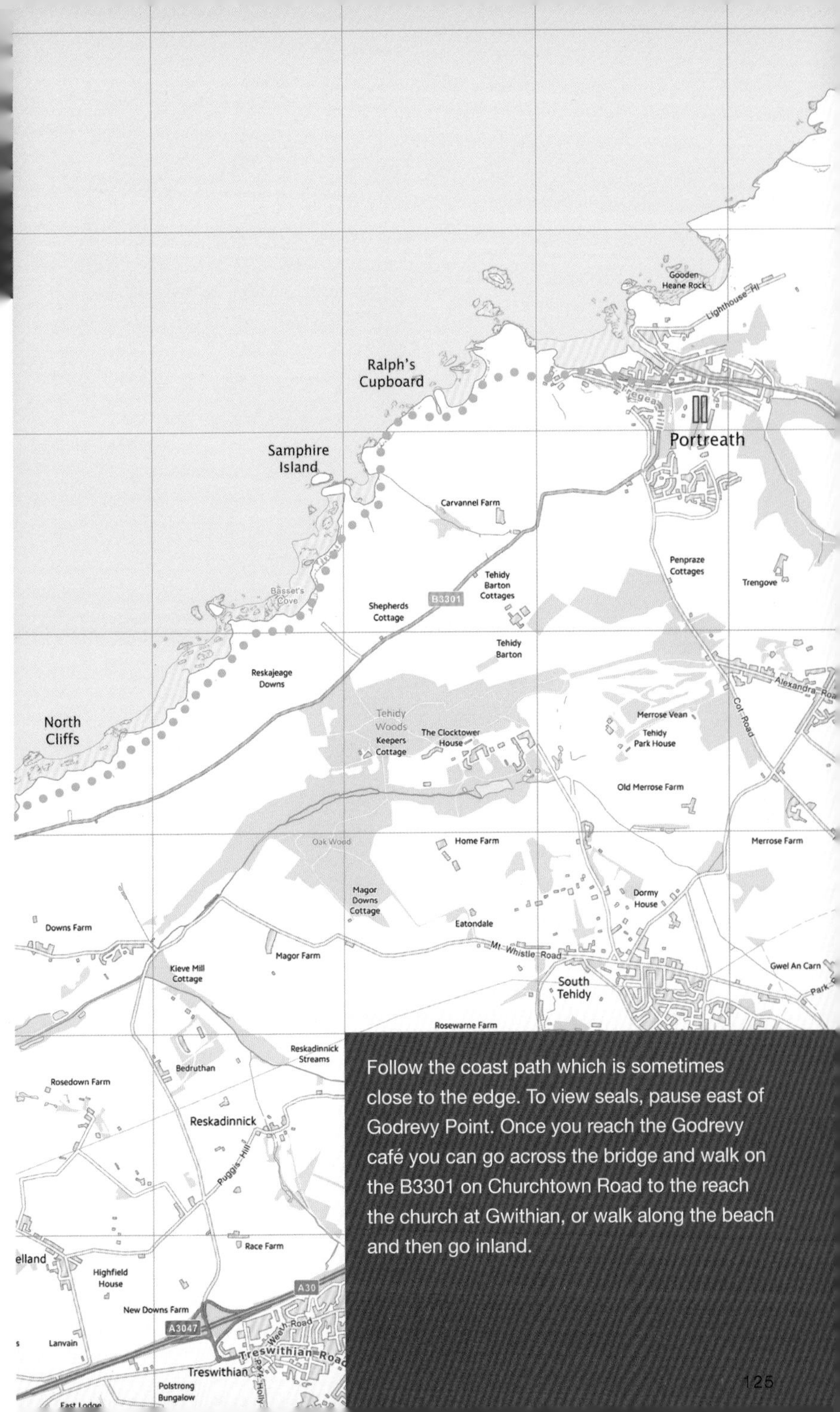

Follow the coast path which is sometimes close to the edge. To view seals, pause east of Godrevy Point. Once you reach the Godrevy café you can go across the bridge and walk on the B3301 on Churchtown Road to the reach the church at Gwithian, or walk along the beach and then go inland.

personal reflection

After the struggle, then comes respite; after the storm, the calm; after challenge, ease. After Portreath there is one more large descent and ascent, the path then smooths out and becomes a flat, easy path, close to very steep drops and the magnificent views from Reskajeage Downs and North Cliffs. You can look back past the circular ball of the satellite listening station. Just before you get to North Cliffs, you come to and stand above a cove with a cave called 'Ralph's Cupboard' - a storehouse for pirate Ralph's smuggling.

I was interested that one of two islands just off the coast is called 'Samphire Island' and was indeed a source of the samphire herb, used in fish dishes. The bright yellow gorse was just coming into bloom, and as my walk was undertaken in springtime, I was watching things emerge and come to life, surrounded by shearwaters, gannets, seagulls and accompanied by bird song.

'Is it safe here?' asked Olaf, the German walker, as he sat with me for lunch on the picnic tables at the 'Hell's Mouth Café'!

I had travelled through a huge range of landscape and emotion: tough walking, then facing the struggles and wilderness, and then many miles on an easy straight path with stupendous views and perilous cliff edges along North Cliffs. Just when I thought that the Celtic trail had gone cold or even dried up, I was delighted to encounter a whole family of Celtic saints and outpouring of missionary endeavour at Gwithian.

On reaching Godrevy, beautiful sands stretch out for miles and I wondered if the Celtic saints believed that they had come ashore in heaven! There is a seal colony at Godrevy (although they were all resting on my visit). The Godrevy lighthouse, made famous in Virginia Woolf's novel *'To the Lighthouse'*, becomes your goal, which seems like a good target. The joy of this part of the walk, when you are able to see and appreciate beauty all around you, is 'a light' for your way and 'a light for your whole body' too.

I found St Gothian's church at Gwithian to be another 'treasured find' after the long trudge over the past two days. Having thought about 'angels ministering in the desert' all along this section of the walk, I was amazed to find a large poster displayed in Gwithian Church about the role of angels, confirming that I had been indeed been on the right track throughout the whole day. The poster read: 'Angels are with you and watch over you whatever you do'.

There is also a Celtic cross for you to touch in the middle of Gwithian churchyard. Gwithian also has an early Methodist chapel established in 1810 close by the church.

christian reference

Jesus said: 'The eye is the lamp of the body. If your eyes are healthy, your whole body will be full of light.' *(Matthew 6:22).*

godrevy lighthouse

Godrevy lighthouse is now an automatic lighthouse and was built in 1859 after there had been many wrecks on the treacherous rocks, including the a packet-steamer, *'The Nile'* in 1854. Many shipwreck victims are buried in Gwithian churchyard.

st. gothian

St. Gothian was an Irish missionary martyred in the area, Charles Thomas' local history book tells us. Grass-marked pottery on the underside of cooking pots and platters very similar to ones used in north east Ireland have been discovered nearby so scholars are able to be fairly accurate about St. Gothian's dates. John Leland discovered a town 'Conertown', buried beneath the extensive sand-dunes in 1540.

St. Gothian was among a band of missionaries who landed with St. Fingar/St. Gwinear at Hayle. Legend has it that they might have been part of a large contingent of 770 men and women as well as seven bishops - or a smaller contingent of four men and three women! However numerous the contingent, or whether these tales are records of separate missionary endeavours, this missionary enterprise met with a sticky end at the hands of the local Cornish king. The arriving saints travelled inland, going up the Roseworthy Valley to 'Conetconia' (now called 'Connor Downs'). The very next day they were set upon by soldiers of a local tyrant called King Teudrig or Teudar who lived at a fortified castle at Riverer, Phillack. St. Gothian was murdered. The name *'Teudar'* means a *'gift of God'* and Teudar himself may have been a Christian and, as other evidence demonstrates in West Cornwall, the area may have been Christianised before the Irish missionaries arrived. King Teudar attacked the Irish missionaries because the Irish were traditionally seen as 'the sea-raiding enemies of the British'. As historian, Catherine John, said: 'he

was well dug into the life of his land and resented intrusion'. Henry Jenner had commented to G.K. Chesterton that the Irish missionaries were not martyred by heathens but by 'rather slack Christians'. Gwithian Church was erected on this site and was dedicated in St. Gothian's honour to mark his martyrdom on his arrival in Cornwall. Also, a holy well at map co-ordinate OS 5882 4180 could have been dedicated to St. Gothian. St Gothian's Chapel, which may have been abandoned due to an influx of sand, was rediscovered in 1827 with the masonry altar intact, but a local farmer called Hockin subsumed it into a farm building and made it into a cowshed. The name St. Gothian was changed to become *'Gwythyen'* in 1567 and *'Gwythian'* by 1601.

St. Gothian's companions included- St. Gwinear, St. Breaca, St. Elwyn, St. Piala and St. Crewenna, St. Crowan, St. Sinnius (the abbot who gives his name to nearby Sithney) and St. Uny. The saints courageously continued in their mission.

St. Gwinear

St. Gwinear gave his name to the church, well and village inland. On his arrival in Ireland, St. Patrick converted the pagan Irish King Clito. Clito's son was called St. Fingar/St. Guinger/St. Gwinear, who had been a hermit in Brittany for a while, living off acorns for food, before he returned to Ireland to lead this large missionary contingent to Cornwall. St. Gwinear is said to have had the ability like Moses to strike a rock and cause water to gush forth and on one occasion to cause three fountains to come out of the ground: one for himself, one for his dog and one for his horse! A spring at nearby Roseworthy is also known as Venton Winear and St. Gwinear is remembered for having restored a cow to life. After his beheading by King Teudar, St. Gwinear is said to 'have picked up his head and carried it away' to the place where the present church in Gwinear is sited today. A tree is said to have grown out of his place of execution and earth taken from his tomb could cure diseases. These tales of St. Gwinear and his missionary companions are recorded in the late thirteenth century *'Life of Gwinear'* written by Anselm, a Breton monk. This is the only complete *'Life'* of a Cornish saint in existence. St. Gwinear is also remembered in Pluvigner in Brittany.

The fate of St. Gothian and St. Gwinear, together with that of the Irish virgin Derwe, whose chapel stood on the site of her murder at 'Menadarva' just over a mile away, show the cost of the Irish mission to Cornwall. St. Gothian, as he saw the golden stretch of sands before him on his arrival here, may have believed that he had arrived in paradise, but it was not to be long before he went to the greater heaven.

St. Breaca

St. Breaca may have been a nun in Ireland at a convent founded by St. Bridget and may also have been a midwife. St. Breaca escaped the wrath of King Teudar and established her cell (now the village of Breage) with her friend St. Germoe close to Tregonning Hill near Helston.

St. Elwyn

Close to the village of Breage, another of St. Breaca's companions, St. Elwyn, gives his name to Porthleven *'porth'*: landing place/harbour, *'leven'*: a derivation of *'elwyn'*. A chapel was dedicated to St. Elwyn at Porthleven and later, a church in the expanding Victorian port of Hayle near where St. Elwyn landed with his companions.

Christian Reference

O Lord Jesus Christ,
Who callest to thee whom thou willest
and sendeth them wherever thou
chooseth
we thank you for sending your servant
Gothian
to preach thy gospel in this parish
and we humbly pray thee to raise up
among us
these heralds and evangelists of your
kingdom. Amen. *(Prayer for St Gothian's Feast, November 1st)*

the path i walk
christ walks it,
may the land in which i
am be without sorrow.
may the trinity protect
me wherever i stray.
bright angels walk with
me - dear presence -
in every dealing,
may every path before
me be smooth
man, woman and child
welcome me
a truly good journey
well does the fair lord
show us a course, a path.

attributed to st. columba d.597

chapter 14

shifting sands

gwithian - lelant

DISTANCE: 6.5MILES/10.5KM | TIME: 3HOURS | DIFFICULTY: EASY

gwithian to lelant

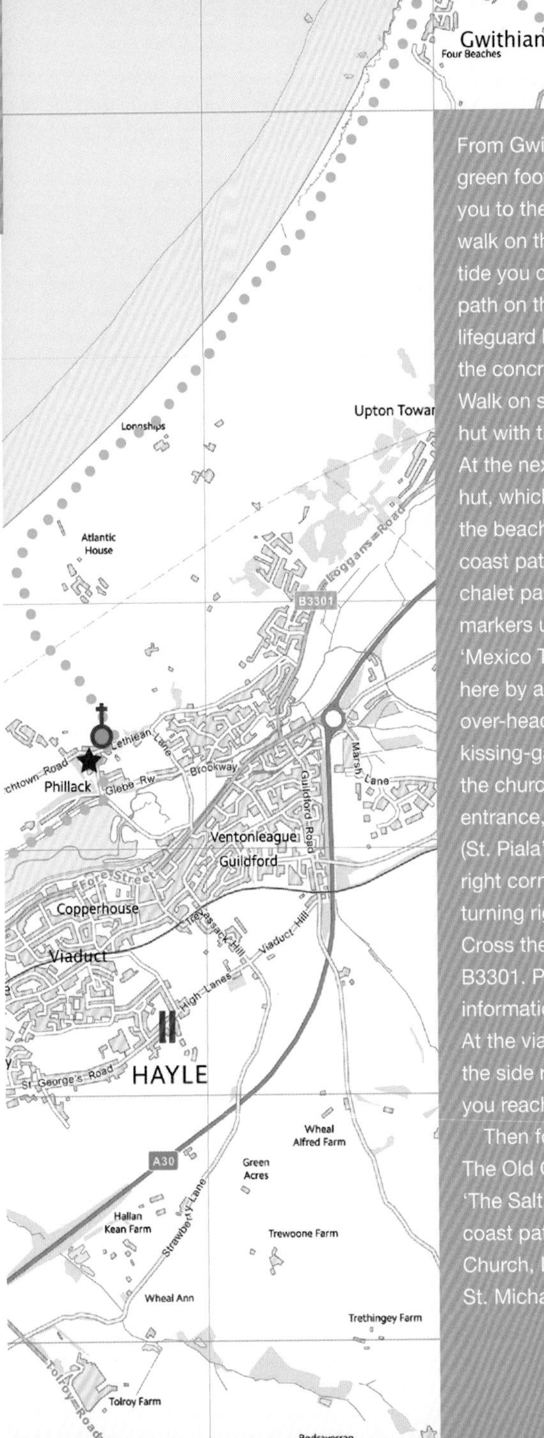

From Gwithian Church follow the green footpath sign which leads you to the coast path. If possible, walk on the beach but if it is high tide you can walk along the coast path on the dunes. Look out for the lifeguard huts- the first one is above the concrete steps at Gwithian Beach. Walk on some distance, noting the hut with the sandy slope to the beach. At the next (Beach View) lifeguard hut, which has wooden fences to the beach, find (or stay on) the coast path in the dunes, skirting the chalet park, following the large slate markers until you find the slate saying 'Mexico Towans'. Go further inland here by a kissing-gate, under some over-head cables, through another kissing-gate and on until you reach the churchyard. Outside the church entrance, cross to the steep road. (St. Piala's well is just inside the top right corner of the hedge.) Go down, turning right along St. George's Walk. Cross the bridge and go right at the B3301. Pass the engine sculpture and information about Richard Trevethick. At the viaduct go past ASDA and take the side road close the estuary until you reach Tempest photography.

Then follow the B3301 round, past The Old Quay House Inn. Go down 'The Saltings' road, go up and rejoin coast path, following signs to St. Uny Church, Lelant and the beginning of St. Michael's Way.

hayle estuary

christian reference

Jesus sent them out to proclaim the kingdom of God and to heal those who were ill. He told them: 'Take nothing for the journey - no staff, no bag, no bread, no money, no extra shirt.' *(Luke 9:2-3).*

personal reflection

This is a walk on a beautiful long stretch of sea-swept, golden sands. It was very clean when I visited, with just a few discarded objects thrown up by the sea: a lobster pot, a piece of driftwood, a large green fishing net. So often, in life I want to wipe the slate clean, to start afresh just like a sea-washed beach, wanting to discard and disregard, to cast off all that burdens. The driftwood symbolised, for me, how we can feel trapped by maintaining houses, properties and possessions; the lobster-pot, a sense of being cooped up and trapped; and the net, being caught in a web. Although I have lived a life of relative simplicity throughout this pilgrimage, staying in a small caravan much of the time, and have left behind the clutter and chaos of competing demands that make up modern life, I'm afraid that I have to admit that this is not anything like the radical simplicity and trust of heart that Jesus proposed to his disciples. I have my trusty staff beside me, a backpack on my back, sandwiches prepared earlier and a drink for lunch, and a wallet too! The only way I follow Jesus' instructions is that I haven't got an extra shirt, but I have got my coat which I needed too, as it rained on this long trek on the sands. During the course of this walk I have shed many pounds in weight (half a stone) and also shed the many toxins acquired of over-exposure and over-yearning on my own part to meet people's needs and expectations and demands.

questions

What would you wish to discard? What binds you? What would you like to leave behind and be free from? When you return from this pilgrimage, will you endeavour to continue to choose a life more of simplicity and openness to the provision of God than previously? What will have shifted within you? What will you dispense with?

personal reflection

I had a rare treat and opportunity on my visit here: after joining the estuary walk to the 'Tempest' factory, I was amazed to see the water in this tidal estuary so very low, that like St. Ia, I gained my heart's desire, and set off across the sands (sometimes the sands were very soft) and crossed the river with the water just up to the top of my wellies. I was able to go across the estuary to the Lelant Railway Station. I felt like one of the early Celtic saints just arriving on the sands of Hayle! Since then, locals have warned me of the quicksand dangers and were horrified that I crossed the estuary, so this is not the route I recommend.

st. felec and st. piala

The name of Phillack may be a combination of these two female Celtic saints' names or they could in fact be the same person. St. Felec was a holy virgin living in a cell by the shore at Phillack whom St. Gwinear met on his arrival in Cornwall. St. Piala was the sister of St. Gwinear and the daughter of Irish King Clito and part of the early missionary endeavour landing at Gwithian. St. Piala had refused marriage in Ireland, took a vow of virginity and left for Cornwall. In the south porch is a *'chi-rho'* cross which may have been associated with St. Piala and the holy well just down from the church. St. Piala was also martyred by King Teudar. In the Middle Ages, the dedication of Phillack Church was Romanised and changed to St. Felicity, a rich widowed mother of Rome with seven sons who were also martyred.

song

Bind us together, Lord,
Bind us together
With cords that cannot be broken.
Bind us together, Lord,
Bind us together,
O bind us together with love.
(Extract taken from the song 'Bind us together' by Bob Gillman, 1977 Copyright(c) Thank you Music)

st. ia, st. uny, st. anta and st. erth

St. Uny Church is a great start to the final leg of the journey, a fine start to the St. Michael's Way pilgrimage route. It was Richard Fitzgerald of Ludgvan Lees, who was related to William the Conqueror, who built the Norman church on this site in 1100 that was connected to the monks of Tywardreath. The clock above the door of the church covers the spot where a statue of St. Uny would have been placed, but this was a family mission and all four siblings are depicted in the fine 1973 stained glass window above the altar, together with St. Gwinear and St. Winwaloe, who preached at nearby Towednack where the church is dedicated to him. Local birds: woodcock, chough, puffins and gulls, a Celtic cross, Trencrom Hill and the seats of the Praed and Tyringham families, who restored the church, are also depicted in this glorious window. It is truly something to behold!

Doble is effusive in praise of these saints: 'They braved the fury of the seas and the elements in their frail craft to bring the gospel to these shores. They set up chapels and wells near rivers or the seashore'. These saints would have arrived at a bustling port at Lelant: tin, gold and ornaments were traded with the Veneti in 325. Jim White in his local history booklet says: 'Lelant would have been a very busy, prosperous, commercial port, where cargo was unloaded to avoid the perilous rocks of Lands End, to be carried on horseback across the tiny isthmus to Marazion'.

St. Ia

St. Ia was a maiden of noble birth born in 430, was converted by St. Patrick in 454 and may also have been a disciple of St. Finnbarr/St. Barry. The legend has it that St. Ia/St. Hya shed many tears when she missed the boat for the expedition to Cornwall from Ireland. She cried so much that her tears fell on an ivy leaf, which miraculously enlarged and expanded to become the size of a small boat (this could have been a coracle like St. Petroc and St. Carantoc used). This leaf bore St. Ia across the seas from Ireland to Cornwall. She settled a little way inland on the land of a well disposed king or chieftain called Dinan, who built her a church. It was there that St. Ia established her cell and gave her name to St. Ives and the wishing well at 'Venton Ia' near Porthmeor Beach. Her tomb was in St. Ives Church in Medieval times. Lanivet Church has also adopted St. Ia as the patron saint and nearby Wendron is a derivation of St Ia's name: *'eglosiga'*: the church of St. Ia. A chapel and holy well is also dedicated to St. Ia in the village of Troon near Camborne.

St. Uny or St. Euny

St. Uny was the brother of St. Ia, St. Anta and St. Erth, and was one of the Irish missionaries who landed with St. Gwinear in the Hayle Estuary. St. Uny, as well as being the patron saint of Lelant, is also patron of Redruth, Crowan and Sancreed. At Redruth, St. Uny converted the chief who ruled on Carn Brea. The well at Sancreed is dedicated to St. Uny and is known as the 'healing springs of St. Uny' that is credited with having the ability to 'dry humours and heal wounds and sores', as my predecessor as the Rector of Ludgvan, William Borlase, wrote in his *'Natural History of Cornwall'* in 1758. The holy well is said to have especially powerful properties on New Year's Eve and on the first three Wednesdays in May! There is also another well close by here: the wishing well at 'Venton Uny'. St. Uny was martyred in battle at 'Merthy Uny' which is now called 'Maronney' at Wendron near Helston on 1 February, and his feast day is still celebrated. St. Uny is also remembered at Plevin and Plouyé in Brittany.

St. Erth

St. Erth/St. Erc/St. Ercus *(414-524)* could have been the St. Erc converted and baptised by St. Patrick, when as a courtier he stood up in reverence at St. Patrick's arrival to the court of King Laoghaire. St. Erth later became Bishop of Slane. St. Erth travelled further up the river to where the village is that now bears his name.

st. anta

St. Anta may well have set up a chapel at Black Rock, 'Chapel Aingar', the rocky point at the mouth of the River Hayle, and her light served as a warning to local mariners as they approached the river and estuary mouth. The chapel was still standing in 1500 and was recorded in *'Bishop Redmayne's Register'*. St. Anta gives her name to Lelant and was a virgin nun. The church at nearby Carbis Bay is dedicated to her.

questions

This family mission makes us ponder how individualised we have become as people. Would you ever undertake a task together as a family? Sometimes families do work together when they run a business or a shop or go off camping together. What more could we achieve if we lived less individual lives and worked more collectively for a common purpose as this great family of saints demonstrated? Who has God given us to work with as 'brothers and sisters' to achieve a common goal or good?

personal reflection

St. Uny Church has had a constant battle with the sand and was covered by a sand invasion in 1538 and 1607. This sand incursion also affected the churches of Gwithian, Perranzabuloe and St. Enodoc, near Rock. The influx of sand also clogged and silted up Lelant Harbour. Between 1679-1834 St. Uny Church had no resident vicar. Salvation Army leader William Booth's mission to Lelant in 1872 led to a restoration of the church, but in 1892 St. Uny Church was still being used as a storehouse for smuggled French brandy - no-one was said to ever visit the church on a weekday!

questions

Sands can blow in and be used to cover up a multitude of sins and not provide us with a clean slate at all! In your life, when have you become clogged or silted up? What has threatened to overwhelm you? When searching for personal fulfilment and happiness, have you become satiated with consumerism? How can you work more collectively with others (family or otherwise) towards the common good?

action

There are five Celtic crosses in the churchyards! Touch each in turn which I chose to link to each of the key saints that are celebrated at St. Uny Church: St Ia, St. Erth, St. Uny, St. Anta and also St. Gwinear. St. Uny Church once had a grave cover carved with scallop shells used by pilgrims.

Tender, could we learn
once more to run
as lovers
landing soft
with tender feet?

To take off our shoes
and run barefoot to
trust our toes
and sift the sand
sense the stones and
take the shred, the bruise and cut
to feel red soil pulse again
and run as our ancestors ran
so light on earth's dust skin;
and beginning of some sweet recovery
and the shedding
of more than shoes,
the softening
of more than tread.

Ian Adams, Run Barefoot, Unfurling, 2014

chapter 15

giants and shells

lelant - carbis bay - ludgvan

DISTANCE: 2.5MILES/4KM | TIME: 1.75HOURS | DIFFICULTY: CHALLENGING

lelant to knill's monument

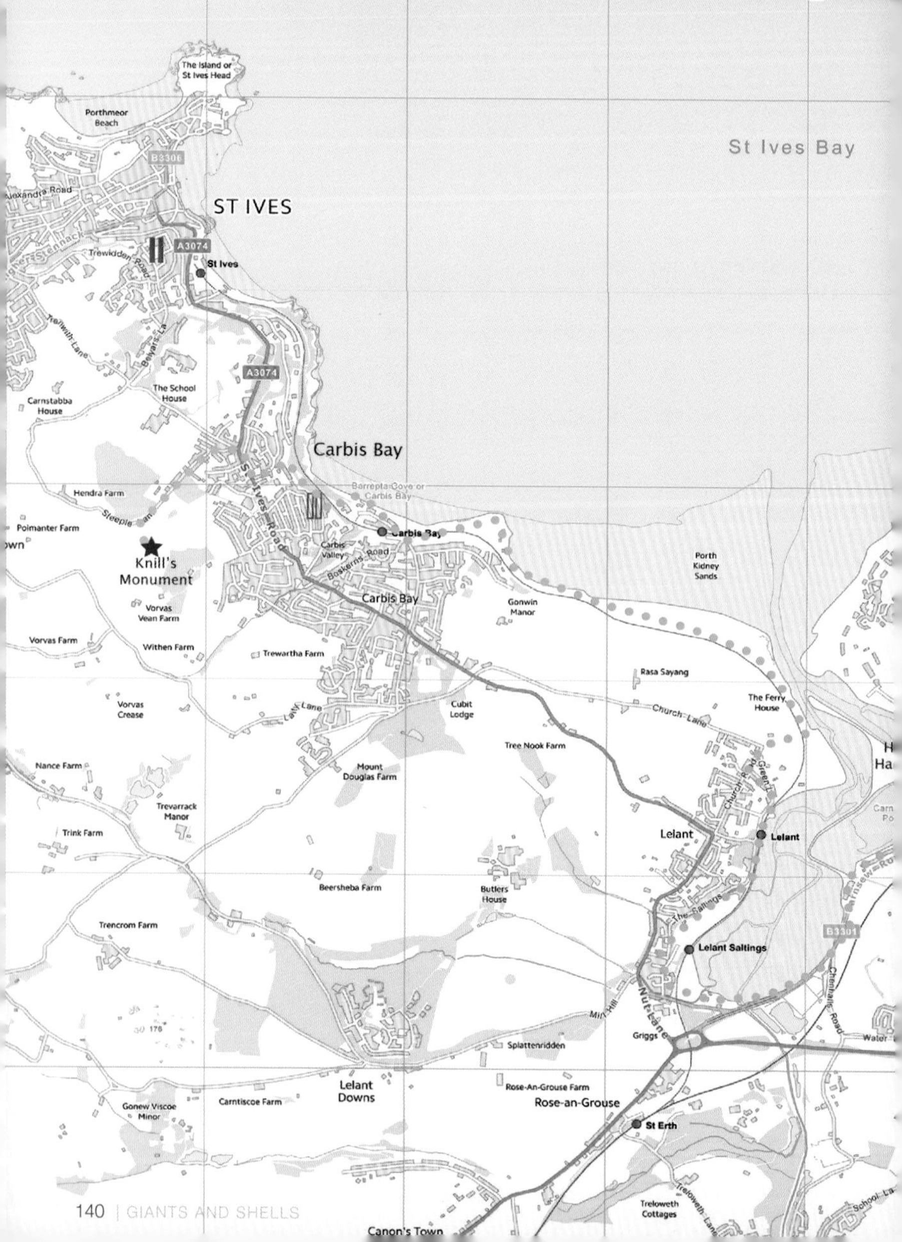

The Cornish Celtic Way route now joins St. Michael's Way, clearly marked by the scallop shell way markers. Start along the footpath by St. Uny Church. Pass under the railway before turning left along a pleasant, narrow dune path overlooking Porth Kidney Sands, that is also the coast path. Just before the top of the climb next to the railway, the coast path forks right, to take you around the (Carrack Gladden) headland. In dangerous windy weather you can continue straight on and stay close to the railway to avoid the exposed headland. You would then rejoin the coast path just below the railway bridge as you walk down the pavement towards the beautiful sands of Carbis Bay. (This is a very sheltered bay and great for swimming and paddle-boarding.)

Once you arrive at Carbis Bay Hotel with its cafe facilities, you follow the coast path around the hotel swimming pool leading to another railway bridge. Look out for the sharp left turn with the scallop shell sign, and go up the steep incline of Wheal Margery Lane. You are passing through an area once rich in minerals which had a working tin mine in 1770, with a shaft running under the seabed.

Throughout you will see Knill's Monument on the skyline, drawing you on forward. Go right and walk on 100m when you reach the main road (A3074) towards St. Ives. At the 'Cornish Arms' pub, turn left onto Tregenna Road and immediately left again into Steeple Lane. Follow this road up the hill to the clear road sign left to Knill's Monument.

action

As you walk along, imagine the arrival of the family of saints: St. Ia, St. Anta, St. Uny and St. Erth, in their coracles on the beautiful stretch of sand. Look across to Godrevy Lighthouse and then nearer to Black Rock, over the other side of the Hayle estuary. Imagine St. Anta's chapel there with its perpetual light and warning to seafarers. Look out for the sixth green of the golf course, where in the 1800s, the cutting for the railway discovered skeletons and a building of Irish origins.

christian reference

Jesus said: 'I am the light of the world. Whoever follows me will never walk in darkness, but will have the light of life'. *(John 8:12).*

questions

Inspired by this family of early saints who brought the light of the Gospel to Cornwall and by how they maintained the chapel light as a guide giving inspiration and hope to many down the centuries, how might the light of Christ be kept alive in our own day? Who will be bearers of Christ's light and Gospel in our own age?

song

This little light of mine, I'm gonna let it shine.
This little light of mine, I'm gonna let it shine.
This little light of mine, I'm gonna let it shine,
Let it shine, let it shine, let it shine.
Hide it under a bush? Oh no!
I'm gonna let it shine........

knill's monument

Knill's Monument is a triangular pyramid of hewn granite 166m (543 feet) above sea level erected in 1782 by John Knill, the Collector of Customs at St. Ives, either because he didn't like the practice of churchyard burials or because he was trying to protect and provide a gateway into St. Ives Harbour. It has served as a navigational aid to seamen ever since. From 1801 there has been a ritual on the feast day of St. James (25 July) every fifth year: ten girls dressed in white dance around the monument to the Furry Dance and Psalm 100 is sung.

st. james and pilgrimage

It is believed that after Jesus' death, one of his closest friends, St. James, (the fisherman brother of St. John) travelled on mission to Spain and died there. His shrine has been visited since the ninth century. Santiago de Compostela became a major source of Medieval pilgrimage; a tradition that has been revived. His symbol is the scallop shell. St. Michael's Way is part of the route to Santiago de Compostela in Spain. This route was taken by pilgrims from Wales and Ireland, avoiding the treacherous rocks at Lands End. There are other ports which were part of these pilgrim journeys, at Fowey and on the Roseland Peninsula.

St. Michael's Way was established in 1994 by the Cornish Pilgrims of St. James of Compostela (*'Bretheren San Jago'*), Cornwall Council and the Cornish Bureau for European Relations. In 1987 the Council of Europe declared a European Cultural Initiative: 'to promote the Santiago de Compostela Pilgrim Way as a highly symbolic and significant European Cultural Route' representing 'a collective memory, overcoming

Take my little light round the world,
I'm gonna let it shine........
Stephen M. Lee

distances, frontiers and language barriers'.

'Our aim is to develop in the citizens of Europe a profound sense of continuity, coming together and exchanging thoughts in the service of European unification.' *(Marcelino Oreja, Secretary General of the Council of Europe).*

Ian Bradley comments: 'there was a widespread desire to recover and celebrate Europe's spiritual roots and soul. As we walk together and travel together, despite our demonstrably different national differences, we can bond together'.

personal reflection

My hope is that the Cornish Celtic Way might bring together those of different nations and faiths, so that they might walk together side by side. It could become a path of encounter of one another, enabling mutual understanding and peace.

poem

Give me my scallop shell of quiet,
My staff of faith to walk upon,
My scrip* for joy, immortal diet,
My bottle of salvation,
My gown of glory (hopes true gage)
And thus I'll take my pilgrimage.
(Sir Walter Raleigh , 1552-1618) (*backpack)

Carbis Bay
Barrepta Cove or Carbis Bay
Carbis Bay
Hendra Farm
Steeple Lane
St Ives Road
Knill's Monument
Polmanter Farm
Halsetown
Culver House
Polmanter House
Bussow Reservoir
Carbis Valley
Boskerris Road
Carbis Bay
Vorvas Vean Farm
B3311
Vorvas Farm
Withen Farm
Penrose House
Trewartha Farm
Vorvas Crease
Laity Lane
Old Holiday Park
Nance Farm
Mount Douglas Farm
Higher Penderleath Farm
Trevarrack Manor
The Count House
Bolenna
212
Trink Hill
Trink Farm
Beersheba Farm
The Bowl Rock
Cripplesease
Trencrom Farm
Chylasson Farm
Brunnion Studios
Booby's Castle
Carne Farm Cottage
Fort Trencrom Hill
176
Polpeor Villa
Nancledra
Ninnes Bridge
Gonew Viscoe Minor
Carntiscoe Farm
Lelant Downs
Trembethow Manor
Red River
Trembethow
B3311
Locke Stampys
Ashtown Farm
Doormouse Cottage
Canon's Town
Ford
Collorian Cottages
Whitecross
Cucurrian Farm
Red River
Cargease Farm
Boskennal
Cockwells La
Cockwells
Trenowin Farm
Tregender Manor
Gitchell Lane
Menwidden Farm
Nanceddan Farm
B3309
Treassowe Manor
Blowing House Hi
Tregender Vean Barn
Tregender Lane
Lower Tregender
Trevorrow Farm
Angwinack Cottage
Vellanoweth
Parc-An-Camps
Little Treassowe
Castle Road
Ludgvan
B3309
Church Hill
Crowlas
A30
Rospeath Farm

DISTANCE: 7.5MILES/12KM | TIME: 3.25HOURS | DIFFICULTY: CHALLENGING

knill's monument to ludgvan

Follow the clear signage from the monument on the St. Michael's Way track. You arrive at the corner of a lane, turn left following the lane downhill for 3/4 mile passing Withen, Venwyn and Crockers Stile. The road takes a sharp turn to the left, follow this, and then, just before a house and rough lane on the left, leave the road by crossing the granite stile to the right which leads on through the grassy fields of an old holiday park and then to a farm/barn. Walk to the lane, cross it looking for the St. Michael's Way sign to the right. This leads you over a granite stile into a field. Walk directly left across a small corner of the large field over another granite stile by some farm buildings. Turn right along the wide track by the hedge that leads to a stile into a path enclosed by hedges. Pass a couple of cottages and on towards the main road. The Bowl Rock is in a grassy area on the right by the road. Cross the road, find the stile opposite to left of the old chapel building. Climb up through the field to the top left hand corner where there is a stile onto a lane. Cross to the granite stile which leads into National Trust land and follow the path round to skirt the base of the Trencrom Hill fort. Take a path to the summit and then descend to the National Trust car park to the south.

From Trencrom Hill National Trust car park, turn right along the lane, then after a few yards, fork left and down a lane following the St. Michael's Way signs. At the bottom, in front of the cottages, turn right along a gravel driveway passing between the stream and Ninnesbridge Chapel House. Notice the Celtic cross. Follow the stream to a well-signposted stile leading up through fields past Trembethow Farm. Continue to follow the clear signs through the fields, across tracks and eventually through more fields and down a steep slope to a lane. The Red River and the ford are a few yards along the road to the right.

Cross by the bridge at the ford following the St. Michael's Way signpost, taking a sharp left hand turn uphill at the lane junction to pass Boskennal Farm. Go over the stile at the top at the bend in the road and walk on and down, heading for the stile in the centre of the woodland boundary at the bottom of a steep field. Go through what feels like an ancient village site in the woods, and up through fields towards the electricity pylon and eventually to Vellanoweth Lane. Turn left, and after a few yards, by a postbox, follow the signage, right, down to the peaceful Eden Valley. Continue on the path through the wood to arrive at the side of Ludgvan Church.

the bowl rock

the bowl rock

Cornwall is a land of legends inspired by the landscape of swamps and sacred groves. Walter de la Mare, on a weekend visit in the 1920s, thought Cornwall to be 'a haunted land where he would never venture again'. A bishop of Exeter once refused to go further than mid-Penwith because of 'the heathens that inhabited Madron and Lands End'; and this part of Cornwall still has a strong and thriving pagan community today. There are many legends of giants and this one involves the giant Trencrom who was a friend of Cormoran, the giant of St. Michael's Mount. They enjoyed a game of bowls together. This huge, round boulder, The Bowl Rock, is a piece left over from their game. In legend, where there are giants there is also buried treasure: at Trencrom this is guarded by wicked little people called 'Spriggans'.

personal reflection

It is interesting how we react to these tales. They could be dismissed as ridiculous stories from the past, something you might find in a child's nursery rhyme. You might be equally dismissive of some of the more extraordinary tales and miracles attributed to the Celtic saints found along the route. The Celtic Christians had strong faith, but were relaxed in their attitudes towards people of other beliefs. Although they worked hard to convert people to Christianity, by preaching and performing signs and miracles, they were not in a position to argue from a point of strength - theirs was not the dominant faith of the land at the time - the imperial dominance of Christendom came much later. The Cornish Celtic saints respected the pagan holy places that they came across and chose them as sites to establish a church or a sacred well.

song

He who would valiant be
'gainst all disaster,
Let him in constancy
follow the Master.

There's no discouragement
shall make him once relent
His first avowed intent
to be a pilgrim.
Who so beset him round
with dismal stories,
Do but themselves confound
his strength the more is.
No foes shall stay his might
though he with giants fight,
He will make good his right
to be a pilgrim.
Since, Lord, Thou dost defend
us with Thy Spirit,
We know we at the end
shall life inherit.
Then fancies flee away!
I'll fear not what men say,
I'll labour night and day
to be a pilgrim.
(John Bunyan. 1628-88)

christian reference

Jesus said: 'Do not let your hearts be troubled. Believe in God; believe also in me. My Father's house has many rooms; if that were not so, would I have told you that I am going there to prepare a place for you'. *(John 14:1-2).*

trencrom hill

At Trencrom Hill you can see way back to Godrevy lighthouse, towards Gwithian sands where the saints arrived on their coracles and across to St. Ives and the magnificent sweep from north to south coast.

Trencrom was an Iron Age fort constructed in the fourth century BC, had walls for protection up to fifteen feet thick and had sixteen huts within its protective wall. It has never been excavated.

Trencrom is a place of spiritual significance, not just because you can see both coasts in one panoramic view, but because it is still used by Buddhists, pagans and sacred dance gatherings and gives a pilgrim good sight of the final destination: St. Michael's Mount.

personal reflection

Mountaintops and hilltops have a great significance in the Bible stories. They are places of revelation and encounter with the divine. There, Jesus delivered his key teaching, the Sermon on the Mount, with its many 'blessings' and it was on a hillside that Jesus fed the five thousand listeners. Often mountaintops are hidden by fog adding to their sense of mystery and the possibility of divine disclosure. Jesus was shrouded in mist and cloud on hills at his Transfiguration and Ascension, just as Moses encountered God in the fog of Mount Sinai.

christian reference

Jesus took with him Peter, James and John and led them up a high mountain by themselves. There he was transfigured before them. His face shone like the sun, and his clothes became white as the light. *(Matt.17:1-2)*

prayer

Heavenly Father,
we give you thanks for this high mountain where we see your glory from coast to coast.
As we stand on this holy site, bless the land and the way before us.
May our eyes perceive your glory revealed to us today in our pilgrimage with you. Amen.

ninnes bridge chapel

In the late eighteenth and early nineteenth century, Methodism grew exponentially due to John and Charles Wesley's preaching, leadership and their engagement with the concerns of the Cornish tin miners, hence Methodism in Cornwall became very strong.

John Wesley had ridden out on Monday 29 August 1743 with three other men to breathe life into Cornish Christianity; the Anglican Church at the time being locked into the patronage of the local gentry and compromised by the collection of land tithes from local farmers. By seven o'clock he was preaching in St. Ives, which he made his headquarters. In spite of opposition, threats of violence and arrest as a spy, he gradually won people over by persuasion. People flocked to hear him preach in ever greater numbers. Many old barns were converted so that every village and hamlet came to have a chapel.

Much of Cornwall consists of a collection of small dwellings and hamlets built around a farm. The Cornish prefix, *'tre'* means *'farm'*. Methodism owes its success to its family roots. Many centuries previously, Celtic Christianity had flourished as a result of a similar clan-based approach. Newspapers questioned whether or not the Methodist revival was of the 'true faith'! As Methodism has declined rapidly since 1990, many of the chapels have now closed or changed use as here at Ninnes Bridge.

personal reflection

Now, in the twenty first century, the Anglican and Methodist communities work ever closer together, relating to each other as two branches of the one stem. Jesus encourages us not to draw artificial distinctions, to stop seeking to decide who is 'in the body' or 'in the vine' but to leave that to him. Jesus encourages us to remain close to him, to draw our strength from him, 'the one true vine', so that we will bear 'good fruit' to offer to the world.

action

By the stream here (at the site of Ninnes Bridge Chapel) there is a Celtic cross for you to touch.

song

Guide me, O thou great redeemer,
Pilgrim through this barren land;
I am weak, but thou art mighty,
Hold me with thy powerful hand;
Bread of heaven, bread of heaven
Feed me till I want no more;

Open now the crystal fountain
Whence the healing stream doth flow;
Let the fire and cloudy pillar
Lead me all my journey through:
Strong deliverer, strong deliverer;
Be thou still my strength and shield;

When I tread the verge of Jordan,
Bid my anxious fears subside;
Death of death, and hell's destruction
Land me safe on Canaan's side:
Songs of praises, songs of praises,
I will ever give to thee;
(William Williams, 1717-1791)

red river ford

Hindus travel to sites near rivers and describe pilgrimage as 'tirtha', a ford or a bridge to the divine.

prayer

We bless this stream of life from God, and all creatures who drink from it. Revive God's refreshing touch on your life, on your family and on your dreams, so that you may drink down deep the message that God is calling you to new life in him. We bless this river to be a reminder of the ever-present life-giving presence of God who has come to heal all our hurting hearts and will one day pronounce his blessing and heal the whole earth. Amen. *(Russ Parker: adapted)*

personal reflection

As I approached my home village of Ludgvan, through the Eden Valley, it reminded me of T. S. Eliot's poem *'Little Gidding'*: after all my wandering it was as though I was seeing my home for the very first time. I was greeted by a group from Ludgvan School on a birthday party treasure hunt, and I felt very much welcomed back home!

chapter 16

journey's end or beginning

ludgvan - st. michael's mount

ludgvan to st. michael's mount

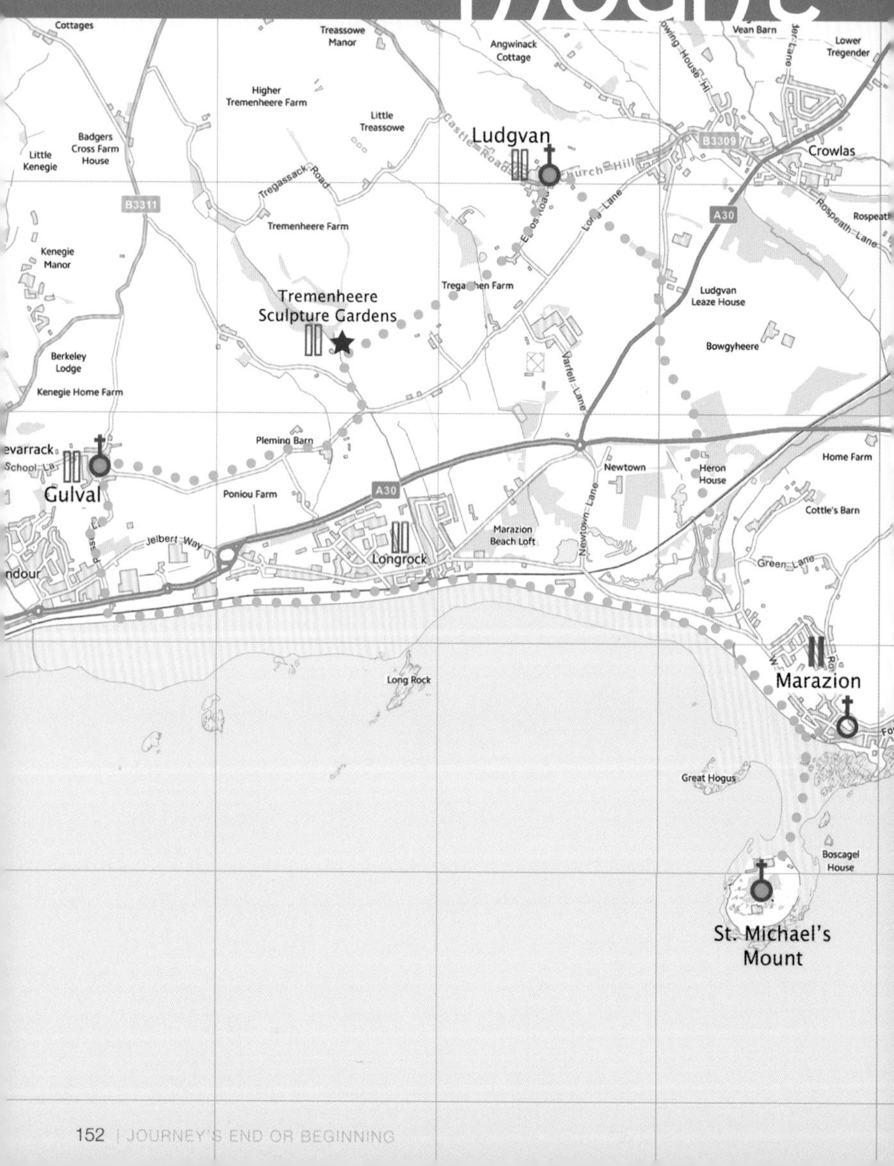

ROUTE 1
through the marshes

DISTANCE: 1.75MILES/3KM | TIME: 0.75HOURS | DIFFICULTY: EASY

Leave Ludgvan Church, turning left and walking past the White Hart pub, and then after Rectory Cottage on the right hand side you will see the St. Michael's Way sign which leads you through beautiful agapanthus and broccoli fields with stunning views of the Mount. Continue down a well cared-for path and find your way to the junction at the A30. Cross the A30 and into the 3 fields of the Tilly's dairy farm, following the signs.

Then across the A395 through to a small pine grove, the marsh, across the railway line and into the Marazion Bird Sanctuary, where you are greeted by birdsong. On arrival at the road, head for the dunes, go across the Red River and walk along the beach to the causeway. Visit Marazion Town, especially All Saints Church and plan your crossing to the Mount.

Looking across Mount's Bay , you can see Penzance, which you can reach by a frequent bus service, or walk the coast path for another 3 miles. There is a steep ascent on the Mount.

ROUTE 2
via gulval

DISTANCE: 4MILES/6.5KM | TIME: 1.6HOURS | DIFFICULTY: EASY

Go right outside Ludgvan Church and then left down Eglos Lane.
At the sharp bend the St. Michael's Way path goes straight on down the side of a cottage, along a hedge. Then down and along, running parallel to the coast. Cross stiles and along tracks to the Tremenheere Sculpture Gardens. The signs then take you to Gulval Church, and from there, take the lane down towards the sea, crossing both the A30 and the railway footbridge. Walk along the coast path or the beach to Marazion and St. Michael's Mount. Note: This route is a good path to take to St. Michael's Mount if the Marazion bird sanctuary is flooded. There is a steep ascent on the Mount.

ludgvan

ludgvan church

In the Doomsday Book, the Manor of Ludgvan Leaze included Ludgvan, Lelant, St. Ives and Towednack. William the Conqueror gave it to his half-brother, Robert Court of Martian, who in turn put it in charge of his steward, Richard Fitzthorold.

'Ludgvan' is thought to be either derived from the Irish name *'Lude-won'* or from St. Luwdegran who was an Irish saint. The circular nature of the churchyard (or *'lan'*) and the close-by well suggest that St. Luwdegran established himself here, probably on a pagan site- a clearing in the woods on a hilltop. We know little else about him, but if you had been baptised in his well, (which has now been built upon in the new housing beyond the telephone box) you could be saved from a hanging! Ludgvan Church became a place of Medieval pilgrimage. Up until the nineteenth century there was a wall-painting of the patron of pilgrims, St. Christopher. Mounted above the door there is a pilgrim with his wide-brimmed hat, satchel and staff.

The White Hart pub next door was constructed as a hostel for the workmen building the 12-14th century church. At Ludgvan, Medieval pilgrims would gather to be lead by 'a good guide' through the perilous woods and marshes (and maybe wolves!) to St. Michael's Mount.

action

Touch and be empowered by the three ancient crosses in Ludgvan churchyard.

personal reflection

I was interested to learn that the last wolf that killed a child in Cornwall was hunted down at nearby Rospeath. Ludgvan Church with its prominent position, has been a source of light, comfort, solace, refuge and rest for many people in the hamlets and farmsteads of this, the largest parish in terms of acreage in Cornwall. Comfort and guidance was also provided by the invention of the Humphry Davy miners' lamp; Humphry Davy's parents farmed at nearby Varfell.

christian reference

I am the good shepherd who is willing to die for the sheep. When the hired man, who is not the shepherd and does not own the sheep, sees a wolf coming, he leaves the sheep and runs away; so the wolf snatches the sheep and scatters them. The hired man runs away because he is only a hired man and does not care about the sheep. I am the good shepherd. As the father knows me and I know the Father, in the same way I know my sheep and they know me. And I am willing to die for them. *(John 10: 11-15).*

The Lord's my Shepherd, I'll not want.
He makes me lie in pastures green;
He leads me by the still, still waters,
His goodness restores my soul.
And I will trust in you alone,
And I will trust in you alone,
For your endless mercy follows me,
Your goodness will lead me home.
He guides my ways in righteousness,
And He anoints my head with oil,
And my cup, it overflows with joy,
I feast on His pure delights.
And though I walk the darkest path,
I will not fear the evil one,
For You are with me, and Your rod and staff
Are the comfort I need to know.
(Extract taken from the song 'The Lord's my Shepherd' by S. Townend, 1996 Copyright(c) Thank you Music)

Thou shalt travel thither, thou shalt travel hither,
Thou shalt travel hill and headland, thou shalt travel down, thou shalt travel up, thou shalt travel ocean and narrow
Christ himself is shepherd over thee,
Enfolding thee on every side,
He will not forsake thee, hand or foot or let evil come nigh thee. *(Avery Brookes)*

personal reflection

There is certainly good land here: just below Ludgvan Church, the land is called 'The Golden Mile', known for its great fertility, yielding two harvests a year. There are flower fields of daffodils and agapanthus and dairy farming too.

christian reference

God has created us and given us this soil, this soil serves as a medium for seed to grow and cattle to graze, it cleans water and regulates climate, it provides warmth, nourishment and support so new life can emerge.
Bless this soil that it may feed and nourish the seed and animals.
Bless those who work this soil and the harvest they produce. Amen.
(Rural Church Network, Yorkshire and Humber, quoted in R. Parker, Rediscovering the Ministry of Blessing, p126)

action - route 1

Feel the strong sense of pilgrimage along this route from Ludgvan Church to Marazion. Pause to admire the spectacular view of the Mount. Perhaps enjoy the sunshine in the pine forest before plunging into the marshland letting the birdsong accompany and be your angel-guide as you approach your journey's end.

St. Gudwal St. Wolvela - route 2

Gulval village could have been named after either or both the saints: St. Gudwal and St. Wolvela. St. Gudwal, a famous monk from Brittany born of 'noble birth' on the British coast, chose to live on a desolate island in the inland sea of Etel where he built a monastery and remained for many years.

Nearby, St. Gudwal's well was used as an oracle to discern if cattle or goods had been lost or stolen and to let visitors know news of absent friends: if the person or goods were in good health, the water is said to have bubbled; if the person was sick, the water was discoloured; if the person had died the water remained still.

St. Wolvela was a sixth century Breton or Welsh saint and nearby Bosulval, '*house of Wolvella*', could mark the place of her hermitage or nunnery.

marazion church

All Saints Church, Marazion is a Victorian church, although there is believed to have been a 'Chapel of Ease' at Marazion, linked to St. Hilary Church, since 1300s. In Marazion Church there is a huge newly commissioned painting and masterpiece by Christian artist, Zoe Cameron, who works nearby at St. Martin on the Lizard. The painting is on the theme of pilgrimage and as well as depicting the vision of the Archangel St. Michael to the fishermen in Mounts Bay in 495, also has smaller pictures inspired by Bible passages. Zoe wishes her painting to be a blessing to all modern-day pilgrims, giving them spiritual food for their ongoing journeys through life.

christian reference

Jesus said: 'I am the bread of life. Whoever comes to me will never go hungry, and whoever believes in me will never be thirsty'. 'Do not work for food that spoils, but for food that endures to eternal life, which the Son of Man will give you.'*(John 6: 35, 27).*

prayer

Lord God Almighty, Ancient of Days, down the generations you walked with our saints as they travelled through the holy and sacred land of Cornwall. We have arrived in Marazion today: come close to us in our pilgrimage of trust with you. As we journey through our lives, and in this church of all the saints, may the people of the way surround us, bind us to you, heal us, release us, restore us, renew us, in the power of the Blessed Trinity: Father, Son and Holy Spirit, Amen.

action

On the beach, you find a treasure trove of pebbles in infinite variety and colour. As you examine them, think of the many pilgrims who have walked this way before us.

As you start on the causeway, look at

Chapel Rock: once there was indeed a small chapel here, like at Polruan and Hayle, with a light dedicated to the Virgin Mary and Saint Catherine.

st. michael's mount

This is the pinnacle and culmination of the Cornish Celtic Way and it is a very fine end. There is lantern cross in the chapel similar to those at St.Wyllow Church, Lanteglos-by-Fowey and at St. Mawgan Church.

Mounts Bay was an important port for the tin trade and was mentioned by the Greek Sicilian geographer Diodorus. Julius Caesar had tried to stop the trade, but Roman interest was rekindled as the milestone (now in St. Hilary Church) in the reign of Constantine suggests. Human beings are entranced by habitable islands. St. Michael's Mount is believed to be part of the lost kingdom of Lyonesse, and it has legends of giants too!

St. Michael's Mount has been a place of Christian pilgrimage, ever since on 8 May 495 when a group of fishermen on a boat saw a vision of St. Michael by the Mount. The Archangel St. Michael is associated with hills and heights and is the protector of travellers and seafarers. In the chapel, the stained glass windows show St. Michael defeating a dragon, symbolic of the devil. *(Revelation 12: 7-8)*

St. Michael's Mount was a Celtic monastery up until 1066, when it came under the Benedictine rule of the Breton monks at the sister island of Le Mont Saint Michel, France. Pilgrims came here to offer a prayer or to perform an act of penance.

personal reflection

On my own journey here, I had to cross the turbulent waters by boat as the causeway was not open, so I imagined the fishermen and their vision as I crossed those choppy waters. I was amazed to be greeted by two friends working as stewards on the Mount – it was such a blessing and confirmation to be greeted by them together!

I have led a Resurrection pilgrimage from All Saints Church in Marazion to the Mount. The chapel on the Mount was the place we read the account of the upper room where Jesus appeared, resurrected, showing Thomas and the other disciples the nail marks on his hands and feet.

action

Look at the John Miller cross, this was his first sculpture. It is as if Jesus is leaping off the Cross, almost in joy, propelling us not to a sense of ending and accomplishment, but willing us, pushing us on and commissioning us to go outside in the service of our needy world. We are not to linger on the mountaintop, but to go into all the world with his message of hope. The end is in fact the new beginning, the next chapter that is to be written in your pilgrimage through life. Truly, the way leads on.

As you study this enlivened figure of Jesus reaching out to the world, take this image with you to survey the horizon from the parapet.

christian reference

Then the eleven disciples went to Galilee, to the mountain where Jesus had told them to go. When they saw him they worshipped him, but some doubted. Then Jesus came to them and said: 'All authority in heaven and earth is given to me. Therefore go and make disciples of all nations, baptising them in the name of the Father and the Son and the Holy Spirit and teaching them to obey everything I have commanded you. And surely, I will be with you to the end of the age.' *(Matthew 28:16-20).*

prayer

Thank you
For the riches,
The golden journey that lies behind,
For the memories, pictures and images,
The loving care for chapels and shrines,
For stones, wells and blessèd companions
The insight, inspiration and stories,
For the overwhelming witness of the saints of the ages.
And the hope we take to our future.
Amen.

action

Read the poem '*Labyrinth*' by Edmin Muir about the road leading onwards from this point.

chapter 17

walking as pilgrimage

reflections on pilgrimage spirituality

how christian pilgrimages began

Christian pilgrimages began with people wanting to walk in the footsteps of Jesus. Jesus was 'the archetypal pilgrim' and was constantly on the move: he was exiled to Egypt as a young child, travelled three times a year to the festivals in Jerusalem, wandered around Galilee preaching and teaching, and finally took the Way of the Cross, 'the Via Delorosa', to his death by crucifixion. After his resurrection, the risen Jesus was on a road again, walking beside his disciples on the road to Emmaus. Koyama claimed that Jesus walked everywhere, 'became slow for us' as walking is the normal pace for humankind. Jesus himself said 'I am the way'. *(John 14:6)* Olive Wynn commented that:

> *'The way of Jesus is a living and a moving way. There is no stagnation. Wherever he was, he was always on the way. We too are called to be 'on the way', on the way that leads to God, the way of utmost love and service to all.'*

In his final speech, Jesus sends out his disciples to heal, preach and teach about the good news of his life and love, and it is Jesus that inspired the Celtic saints to leave their homelands in Wales and Ireland. In Medieval times the three great destinations for pilgrims were Jerusalem, Rome and Santiago de Compostela, but these were not the only holy places of pilgrimage: St Michael's Mount was once a great destination of Christian pilgrimage too.

Pilgrimages were often quests for an intense experience. Perhaps to seek a transcendental encounter with the divine, or to seek forgiveness for a wrongdoing. Pilgrimages were also associated with miracles, and some went on pilgrimage journeys to be healed. The ill and diseased went from shrine to shrine in their quest for health, and felt that by touching or drawing close to the relics or objects associated with holy people they would be healed.

why go on a pilgrimage today?

People choose to go on a walking journey for all sorts of reasons: to see new sights, walk through beautiful landscapes and to learn something of the geography and history of the place. Ian Bradley in his book '*Pilgrimage*' said:

> *'Pilgrimage offers a departure from everyday life in search of spiritual well-being, a sense of adventure, getting out of a rut, to broaden our horizons or to seek new and different experiences.'*

Some are curious, others uncertain what they seek, some go on pilgrimage to fulfil a long held dream or promise. A pilgrimage may arise out of a sense of restlessness, a quest for a deeper spirituality or in order to re-orient one's life, to make a new start or to escape from the mediocrity of the everyday. Robert Fyall wrote:

> *'Our lives can often feel that they are a struggle and we are at a dead end. We can become*

apathetic and in despair. A great black cloud hangs over everything. We take no pleasure in family or friends. And our work has gone stale on us. We have a constant sense of inadequacy, vulnerability and guilt.'

A pilgrimage could be prompted by or follow after a crisis point has occurred in one's life: after the death of a loved one or the collapse of a relationship, or it could be made in order to review the direction of life or for physical and psychological healing. I was going on pilgrimage with the express purpose of seeking to rediscover God in my life and to ask him what my future might hold. I found the pilgrimage to be utterly transformative, hence my enthusiasm to share the experience in this book.

the essence of pilgrimage

The essence of pilgrimage has been described in a number of ways. Fyall claimed that pilgrimage can teach us to see through the outer realities and find significance beyond the apparent meaninglessness of much of our daily lives, to see opportunities for growth in all the hurts, slights and conflicts and to see 'in the grey days of the drab grind and routine, the possibility of wells of water springing up in unexpected places', 'the familiar can obscure the eternal'. Similarly, I found it difficult to locate many of the holy wells.

On pilgrimage we live in the present moment. Spiritual writer, Daniel O'Leary, wrote:

'Once again you are gifted with a whole new day, free of charge, and offered once only, that could be lived in a cul-de-sac of fear or against an infinite horizon. Let today be a day for reaching out in thanksgiving, a day of expansion of your heart, a day for breathing out of your system the suffocating baggage of yesterday and yesteryear. So reflect a while each morning on the power of blessing and praising that we all carry, bless the world and its people with love and compassion, send out blessings to everyone and everything.'

We are naturally nomadically inclined, Bruce Chatwin claimed in *'Songlines'*. The respected travel writer William Dalrymple said:

'Walking by its very nature purges the body and soul, calms the mind, the act of walking can distil ones thoughts so that all the worries that obscure clarity and peace of mind can rise to the surface and become filtered away.'

Mikhaly Csikszentmihalyi called it 'the flow': when we act with total involvement and we lose our ego, our sense of control until little distinction exists between the self and the environment and everything comes together in an unforced harmony.

By walking, cultivation of an attitude of love and gratitude can transform a path of grim struggling: pilgrims bless the land they travel on, as Psalm 84 said: 'As they travelled through the land they made it a place of springs'.

If the pilgrimage has worked its wonders, the pilgrim will come back changed, more compassionate, more open, more free, more faithful, more hopeful, more aware and attuned. Alan Jones said:

'I begin to live from a centre other than my own self-protection, manipulating ego. I begin to move in a new direction. I am sufficiently out of the way that I get a glimpse of what it might mean to love without strings.'

In pilgrimage, Francis Bordeaux said that we have an opportunity to de-centre ourselves. The pilgrim goes out to the other to return as another person. It is a movement of 'the detachment of the self', of self-emptying.

If you travel with others, an egalitarian society is created, where people are freed from hierarchical roles. As Victor and Edith Turner noted:

'I have seen in pilgrimage the only possible classless society. The industrialist, the merchant, the professional man next to the worker, people of different faiths and cultures. On the road they walk, suffer and pray together. In the inns they throw themselves down side by side on the same piece of ground and even dress the same.'

encountering creation

I was so blessed that this pilgrimage took place in April just after Easter. I was walking through the resurrection: new lambs, new buds and new flowers were emerging along my path everyday. I haven't words to describe the beauty of a woodland covered in primroses, or an ancient stile in lichen and moss; how my heart soared with the joy of walking through a field of proud ewes with lambs, innocent and staring, defensive and happy; or when I saw the stoat looking up before darting into the hedge by the flooded path; the robins, pheasants and the owl who accompanied me along the way; nor the sense of walking in the mystic way with the holy, the overwhelming kindness I met from strangers and companions, urging me on, the sense of moving from place to place, where a holy man or woman have left their mark and where the holy of today maintain these wondrous sites, the sense of the blessing in seeing a church tower or spire on the skyline, or the sense of encouragement a way marker or standing cross or stone can give you; the blessing I received from learning and drawing closer to the early saints of Cornwall, or a viaduct in a valley or a smiley 'Give Way' sign; or encountering the preserving philosophy in the futuristic biomes of the Eden Project. Much of this walking route is spent close to the sea with its sense of depth and infinity, vast oceans as far as the eye can see. John Nash said of the main business of the artist:

'To train the eye to see, I have made the habit of looking, of really seeing. What a disaster it would be to pass through this one and only earthly life and miss its glories.'

As I walked along I rediscovered that creation was not depraved, dangerous, other, to be conquered and beaten underfoot, lesser, unyielding, fallen or evil, but a source of grace and blessing. Beauty became a gateway to the transcendent, and the landscape sacramental: As the poet William Blake said 'everything that lives is holy' and was 'charged with the grandeur of God' according to Gerald Manley Hopkins. The landscape and the things in it are not dead, but became living companions that accompanied me on my journey too. As human beings, we come from 'adam' (meaning 'earth'), we are of the same carbon essence as every life form and so are not so separate from it. We all are shoots from the one tree of life mentioned in Genesis. As Tagore said:

> *'The same stream of life that runs through my veins night and day runs through the world. It is the same life that shoots in joy through the desert of the earth and the numberless blades of grass and breaks into tumultuous waves of leaves and flowers.'*

Spiritual writer, Daniel O'Leary added that: 'Christianity has always been a great champion of the mystical intimacy at the heart of nature, of the indwelling of the holy spirit of energy, of the brightness of the divine artist in everything that exists'. This was also how the Celtic saints experienced the world as spiritual writer, Philip Sheldrake said:

> *'These frontier or boundary places were sometimes associated with traditional sacred places such as woodlands, wells, oak groves, rivers, springs, clearings in the forest, tribal burial places, cemeteries, mountaintops, and are 'doorways from this material world into the spiritual.'*

To be immersed in creation there was also a feeling of homecoming, beautifully expressed by C.S. Lewis:

> *'The new one (Narnia) was a deeper country: every rock and flower and blade of grass looked as if it meant more. It was the Unicorn who summed up what everyone was feeling. He stamped his right fore-hoof on the ground and neighed and then cried: 'I have come home at last! This is my real country! I belong here! This is the land that I have been looking for all my life though I never knew it until now. The reason why we loved the old Narnia is that it looked something like this.'*

seeking the destination

In life, I hunger to know the end: to try to work out what will be the outcome in a particular presenting dilemma or the end of the story in a book or film. This is my approach to work too: I think to myself, 'If I only send this one more e-mail at 10pm at night, or sort out this piece of paperwork or solve this problem, only then, once I've got to the end, can I relax because I will have overcome it'. This approach to life can make one truly miserable.

When walking a long distance path and heading for the destination: a landmark, a church, a wayside cross or holy well one can hunker down with blinkers on, and head straight for it without taking notice of the journey. William Henry Davies talked about having time 'to stand and stare' in his poem *'Leisure'*.

In walking, I found that the rhythm of the long distance path and the slowness of the journey made me more open to experiences, changing the way I observed the landscape. These experiences and encounters balanced the need to reach my destination, so that reaching the end was not the all-consuming goal.

I don't agree with R.L. Stevenson's maxim that 'it is better to travel hopefully than to arrive'. The destination remained important, giving a resolution, an arrival, an endpoint; sometimes a holy, thin place resonant with the history of a Celtic saint, sometimes a place that seemed marginal, or on the edge, or irrelevant but was in fact, in the heart of things. The Celtic saint, St Columbanus wrote:

> *'We who are on the road should hasten on, for the whole of life is like one day's journey. Just like pilgrims we should continually sigh for our homeland, for travellers are always filled with hope and desire for the road's end. And, so, since we are travellers and pilgrims in this world, let us think upon the end of the road, that is our life, for the end of the way is our hope.'*

walking with the cornish celtic saints

After the Roman occupation of Britain ceased in 410, the churches on the fringes of the Empire continued to develop in a different way from the Church in Rome based on the tribal and clan societies of Ireland and Wales. They had a keen belief in the Trinity, seeing God as Father, Son and Holy Spirit; and a love of creation, which was expressed through the decoration of their illuminated manuscripts with bees and mice and all manner of creatures in their margins.

They were pioneers, they travelled for God, '*peregrino pro Christo*', often setting off in rudderless boats, 'they knew not where'. The Anglo-Saxon Chronicle in 891 told of three Irish monks who stole a boat without oars because 'they wanted to be in a state of pilgrimage, they cared not whither'. Thankfully, these aspiring and inspiring souls landed in North Cornwall. They chose exile and what the Celts called, 'white martyrdom': exile and separation from the land of their birth and kin, away from the distractions of home. They had a spirit of adventure and discovery and were open to where God was leading them. Philip Sheldrake said they combined their missionary outreach with a personal spiritual quest to find 'their place of resurrection' - the place in which they would give of their energy and lives, and eventually die. As Pemberton concluded: 'No other period in history has seen such a widespread and successful missionary outreach'.

Eleanor Duckett described the austere and physically demanding nature of the Celtic saints' mission and pilgrimages evocatively:

> *'They might be seen sometimes in companies of twos or threes or often alone, tramping along lanes and trails, struggling through forests, plunging through the depths of bog and marsh, climbing the mountains. On their feet they wore sandals of hide: their monkish habit was of skin roughly sewn together, with a hood to protect them from the cold and rain, in their hands*

they carried a staff and from their shoulders hang their pack which held their small store of food, their cup, books of prayer for mass and office. Their food was begged from peasants .... At night they made a bed of boughs upon the open sky, sometimes a cottager gave them lodging in a barn or allowed them to drink some milk from his cow before they left at dawn. A pool or stream by the path on the moor or in the forest was welcome for washing away the stain of travel, and plagues of itching stings and bites gathered in the sun, the woods, in the hay barns amid the straw.'

They left wells, standing stones, chapels and oratories, examples of which can be encountered on this Cornish Celtic Way. Cornish 'holy' men and women may not have been classified as 'saints' by the Church in Rome, but they were called saints by the indigenous people of Cornwall, who took their mission to their heart and named so many places after them. Great miracles and healings were associated with them, some seeming outlandish to modern ears.

As you walk along this pilgrimage route, you might feel as if you are catching something in the wind, just like the 'Bisto Kids' in the old advert, walking in their footsteps and in their strides and becoming, as John Bell sang, 'attuned to what the ancients exposed, proclaimed and wrote'. Martin Robinson asserted that 'the pilgrim becomes a part of a previous multitude, a participant in all that has happened and to become one with all that has gone before'. I felt that the presence of the Celtic saints was immanently around me, blessing me, as I followed in their footsteps and inspiration. These saints can help us to move forward, their roving for 'love of Christ', helps us to see the possibilities in our own lives. Spiritual writer Daniel O'Leary commented that:

'Among our ancestors were giants and champions, slayers of dragons in the arena of courage and love. They faced the wild enemies and they faced their own wild, inner selves. These are the wind beneath our wings, who light the furnace in our souls, who surround us gently when the chill fingers of fear close around our hearts.'

To conclude, the spiritual writer Gerald Hughes wrote about his own pilgrimage:

'As I walked the roads I often thought about the Celtic Christian monks who wandered through Europe and God's creation. At first they were imaginary figures from a distant past but they are in God who is eternal, that is always 'in the now', in the God who keeps my legs going along these roads, so these Christian saints are as near as the living, in fact nearer. Why shouldn't St. Patrick cheer me up on the road as much as the waitress cheered me by lighting a candle at the table?'

acknowledgements

Many people inspired me to pursue this Cornish Celtic Way: particularly David Adam, Ray Simpson, Van Morrison, John Bell and the Iona community, and the Taizé community.

Thank you to my colleagues and the people in the Mounts Bay group of churches, where I currently serve as Rector. Many encouraged and blessed me as I set out on my three-month journey to discover this new way in Cornwall, and now participate in breathing and praying this Cornish Celtic Way into existence.

Thank you to Tim Thornton, the Bishop of Truro and to Chris Goldsmith, the Bishop of St. Germans who have continued to encourage me in the development of retreats and the pilgrimage and have allowed me the time to explore this route. I would also like to thank colleagues, especially Roger Bush and Alan Bashforth, who together with all the Truro Cathedral staff, gave me a prayerful and supportive space in which this book could be written. Thank you to the Diocese of Truro administrative staff who actively promote this Cornish Celtic Way project.

Most of all I would like to thank my wife, Penny, for her faith, belief and unfailing support and shared dreams. Also, my daughter, Rosanna who used her skills, expertise and good counsel to design and direct this book.

Nigel Marns

glossary of saints by chapter

Agnes, 12
Aidan, 10
Anta, 14, 15
Austell, 4
Blaisé, 4
Brendan, 7, 17
Bridget, 3
Breock, 7,9
Breaca, 13
Cadoc, 8, 9
Carantoc, 11
Clement, 7
Columb, 10
Columba, 2, 10, 17
Columbanus, 17
Conan, 1
Constantine, 8
Crewenna, 13
Croidan, 7
Cubert, 11
Cuthbert, 2, 7
Cyor, 5
Dagan, 7
Derwe, 13
Efelwy/Ufelwy, 9
Enodoc, 14
Erth, 14,15
Eval, 9
Felec, 14
Fimbarrus, 4, 14
Germanus, 1, 7, 9
Gudwal, 16
Gulval, 16
Gothian, 13
Goran, 4, 7
Gwinear, 13,14
Hilda, 3
Ia, 6, 14, 15
Ildierna, 3
Illtud, 8
Ingunger, 6
Issey, 7
Ludewon, 16
Mawgan, 9
Medan, 7
Merryn, 8
Nicholas, 2
Nivet, 6
Patrick, 1, 7, 11, 13, 14, 17
Petroc, 7, 11, 12
Piran, 11
Piala, 14
Samson, 5, 7
Sulien, 5
Tudy, 7
Uny, 13
Winwaloe, 1, 4, 14
Wolvela, 16
Wyllow, 3

glossary of cornish words

Chy	*House*
Eglos	*Church*
Gwel	*Field*
Pont	*Bridge*
Porth	*Cove, creek, harbour, landing place*
Tal	*Brow of a hill*
Towan	*Sand dune*
Tre	*Farm*
Wheal	*Mine working*
Lan	*Holy site or holy place*
Vean	*Smaller*
Venton	*Well*

references

Bible References

All biblical references are from The Holy Bible, New International Version (R), NIV (R), Copyright (C) 1973, 1978, 1984, 2011 by Biblica, Inc. TM. Used by permission. All rights reserved worldwide.

Chapter 1

- Philip Sheldrake in *'Living Between Worlds: Place and Journey in Celtic Spirituality'* talks about *'transit points'*, 8
- John Spence describes the doorway in his booklet *'St. German's Church - A History and Guide'.*
- Robert Fyall writes about Abraham and Sarah being 'flawed disciples' in *'Travelling Hopefully'*, SPCK, 1996, 25.
- Extract from the text of *'One More Step along the world I go'* by Sydney Carter *(1915-2004)* (C) Stainer & Bell Ltd., 23 Gruneisen Road, London N3 1DZ, England, www.steiner.co.uk is used by permission. All rights reserved.

Chapter 2

- Read about St. Cuthbert in Bede, *'Life of Cuthbert'*, Chapter 10, 58.
- Philip Sheldrake on 'boundary places', *ibid*, 7.
- J. Finney on the inspiration of the deset fathers in *'Recovering the Past: Celtic and Roman Mission'*, 54.
- The historian A. Hastings is quoted by G. Smith in his *'Introduction: Reviewing Mission in Western Society'* in *'Christian Mission in Western Society'*, 54.
- Read about Joseph of Arimethea in Matthew 27:57, Mark 15:43, John 19:38.
- William Blake's poem *'Jerusalem'* is from *'Preface to Milton, a Poem'*, 1810.

Chapter 3

- The inspiration for this reflection came from Revelation 14:13 'the record of their deeds'.
- Diana Pé's quotation is from Pé, D., *'Cornwall Walks to Churches'*, Downland Print Series, 113.
- The inspiration for the reflection on what one could 'lay down your life for' comes from John 15:13.
- Frances Eileen Burdett talks about the naming of St. Saviour's Church, Polruan in Burdett, F.E., *'The Story of St Saviour at Polruan'*, Pegasus, 2016, 10.

Chapter 4

- The quote about 'messing about in boats' comes from Grahame, K., *'The Wind in the Willows'*, Chapter 1.

Chapter 5

- The reference to Van Morrison's song *'Avalon of the Heart'* is from *'Enlightenment'*, 1990, Exile Productions.
- The naming of Luxulyan Church is discussed in Murray, *'Handbook of Devon and Cornwall'*, quoted in Rowe, J., *'A Short History of Luxulyan Parish and the Parish Church of SS Cyriacus and Juliatta'.*

Chapter 6

- J. Key wrote about standing crosses on Iona and was quoted by Robinson, M., *'Sacred Places, Pilgrim Paths: an Anthology of Pilgrimage'*, 117.
- Jenna Plewes' poem *'The Legacy'* from her book *'Gifts'*, is used by kind permission.

Chapter 7

- J. Norden writing on Withiel burial mounds was quoted by Lewis, H. & G., *'The Saints Way, Card 3'*, St. Breock Downs to Tremore.
- Diana Pé writing on Little Petherick Church in Pé, D., *ibid*, 77.
- Nan Shepherd *(1893-1981)* described the magic of the Cairngorms in her book '*The Living Mountain*' quoted Usher G.B., *'Places of Enchantment: Meeting God in Landscapes'*, 71.
- Daniel O'Leary in his book *'Travelling Light: Your Journey to Wholeness'*, 56.
- Thomas Merton quoted by Daniel O'Leary, *ibid*, 56.
- *David Adam's prayer 'Make me a Blessing' is from 'The Open Gate', 108-9.*
- Extract from *'Brother, sister, let me serve you'* ('The Servant's Song') © 1977 Universal Music - Brentwood Benson Publishing (Adm capitolcmgpublishing.com/UK&Eire Song Solutions www.songsolutions.org) All rights reserved. Used by permission.

Chapter 8

- Jeremy Dowling writes of St. Merryn Church in Dowling, J., *'Church Trails of Cornwall: The Padstow Area'*.
- The story of St. Cadoc's miraculous creation of a well is taken from the fantastical eleventh century *'Life of St. Cadoc'* written by the Welsh monk, Llifris of Llancafarn, 600 years after St. Cadoc's death, recorded in G.H. Doble, *'The Saints of Cornwall'*, Part Four, 58.
- Charles Henderson is quoted by Ray Ramm in his book *'Trevose Golf and Country Club'*.
- R.S.Thomas' poem *'The Bright Field'* from his *'Collected Poems 1945-1990'* is reproduced by kind permission of the Orion Publishing Group.

Chapter 9

- The quote from William Blake is a fragment from '*Auguries of Innocence*', *(1803)*.
- Permission to use the words from Keith Duke on the album '*Sacred Weave*', 2005, by Kevin Mayhew Ltd.
- Permission to use the words from Margaret Rizza, *'In God alone'*, 2014 and *'Calm me Lord'*, 1998, by Kevin Mayhew Ltd.
- *'Very present help in danger'* is from Psalm 46:1.
- Edward Pruen writes of St. Eval Church in Pruen, E., *'A Guide to the Ancient Parish Church of St. Eval, Cornwall'*, 2015, see pages 2-5 and quotes Charles Henderson on page 5.
- Words: *'God is our strength and refuge'* (C) Richard Bewes/Jubilate Hymns. copyright manager@jubilatehymns.co.uk. Used by permission.

Chapter 10

- Becca mac Luigdech, quoted by Ian Bradley in Bradley, I.,*'Pilgrimage: A Spiritual and Cultural Journey'*, 41.
- For the reflection on surfing I was greatly helped by my daughter Rosanna Marns' dissertation *'To what extent do surf brands reflect the culture that underpins surfing?'*, Cardiff

Metropolitan University, BA Hons Graphic Communication, 2015.

- The quote from Duke Boyd is from a 1968 article on soul-surfing in *'Surfing'* magazine cited by Warshaw, M., *'The Encyclopedia of Surfing'*, Orlando, Fla,:Harcourt, 2003, p228.
- Thomas Mitchell is quoted on the website kenrockwell.com , *'Seven Levels of Surfers'*, 2015.
- Ford and Brown's quote is from Ford, N., and Brown, D., *'Surfing and Social Theory'*, London, Routledge, 2006, p30.
- *'The Unbounded Ocean'* from *'Unfurling'* by Ian Adams is (C) Canterbury Press, 2014, used by permission. rights@hymnsam.co.uk.

Chapter 11

- C.R. John talks about St. Carantoc in, *'The Saints of Cornwall'*, 38.
- *'Come to the Well'* and *'St. Piran's Song'* are written by Annie HenryHolland, from the album *'Seven Songs'*, 2017, used by kind permission.

Chapter 12

- Ian Bradley quoted in *'The Celtic Way'*, Darton, Longman and Todd, 1993.

Chapter 13

- *'The Celtic Travelling Prayer'* is from Reith, M., *'God in our Midst: Prayers & Devotions from the Celtic Traditions'*, 1975, 38, quoted by Robinson, M., *ibid*, 56.
- Church Father Origen quoted by Robinson, *ibid*, 131.
- The story of Jesus being ministered by angels is from Mark 1:13.
- Charles Thomas writes about Gwithian in his local history book on Gwithian, 1964, 2.
- C. R. John wrote about Cornish King Teudar and quoted Henry Jenner, *ibid.*, 47.

Chapter 14

- C.H. Doble quoted in local history booklet, *St. Uny Lelant*, 2.
- Jim White on Lelant harbour in his local history booklet, White, J., *'St Uny: Fact or Fiction'*, 6.
- *'Run Barefoot'* from *'Unfurling'* by Ian Adams is (C) Canterbury Press, 2014, used by permission. rights@hymnsam.co.uk.
- Permission to use words from *'Bind us together'* by Bob Gilman *Adm. by Capitol CMG Publishing worldwide excl. UK & Europe, admin by Integrity Music, part of the David C Cook family, *songs@integritymusic.com*

Chapter 15

- Marcelino Oreja quoted in *'St. Michael's Way: Forth Sen Myghal'*. Cornwall County Council, 1994.
- Ian Bradley's comment from Bradley, I., *ibid*, 70.
- The quotation from Walter de la Mare is from Bernard Walke, *'Twenty Years at St Hilary'*, 18.
- The piece about John Wesley comes from the *'St. Michael's Way: Forth Sen Myghal'*, *ibid.*
- The prayer about the stream is from Russ Parker's book *'Rediscovering the Ministry of Blessing'*, 107.
- The prayer about the soil is produced by the Yorkshire and Humber section of The Rural Church Network and was quoted by Russ Parker pg 126 *'Rediscovering the Ministry of Blessing'*,
- Avery Brooke, *'Celtic Prayers'*, quoted by Robinson, M., *ibid*, 155.

- T.S. Elliot's poem *'Little Gidding'* is part of *'The Four Quartets'*.
- Words from Stuart Townend *'The Lord's my Shepherd'*, 1996, *Adm. by Capitol CMG Publishing worldwide excl. UK & Europe, admin by Integrity Music, part of the David C Cook family, *songs@integritymusic.com*

Chapter 17

- Martin Robinson, *ibid*,12, talks about Jesus as the archetypal pilgrim.
- Kosuke Koyama on Jesus walking everywhere is from *'Pilgrim or Tourist'*, 1974, 1-3, *quoted by Robinson, ibid, 49.*
- Olive Wynn wrote on *'The Way of the Pilgrim'* quoted by Robinson, *ibid*, 95.
- Benedicta Ward wrote on the misuse of pilgrimage in *'Pilgrimage of the Heart'*, 9
- The reasons why people chose to go on pilgrimage are described by Ian Bradley in his book *'Pilgrimage'*, *ibid*,11, by Martin Robinson, *ibid*, 1, by C. Pemberton in *'Soulfaring'*, xiv, and by Robert Fyall, *ibid*, 47, 57, 87.
- Martin Robinson describes 'the familiar hiding the eternal', *ibid*, 11 and Robert Fyall tells of the revelatory nature of pilgrimage in *ibid*, 47, 57, 87.
- Daniel O'Leary, wrote on embracing each day in *'Travelling Light: Your Journey to Wholeness'*, 72, 82.
- Bruce Chatwin is quoted by Ian Bradley's book on pilgrimage, *ibid*,20.
- William Dalrymple, on his preparation to be married, is from *'A Pilgrim's Progress Ends'* in *'The Spectator'* magazine, 22 June 1991, 14 and was quoted by Robinson, M., *ibid*, 20.
- Alan Jones is quoted by Robinson, M., *ibid*, 25; Francis Bordeaux from *'Pilgrimage, Eucharist, Reconciliation'*, *'Lumen Vitae'*, 29, 1984, 401, *ibid*, 29; and Victor and Edith Turner, *ibid*, 73.
- The citing of self-emptying is from the Letter to the Philippians 2:7-8.
- The artist, John Nash, is quoted in Michael Mayne, *'This Sunrise of Wonder'*, x.
- The tree of life is mentioned in Genesis 2:9.
- The writer Tagore is quoted by Daniel O'Leary, *ibid*, 67 and the quotation from O'Leary himself is from *ibid*, 66.
- Philip Sheldrake writing on the Celtic saints in *'Living Between Worlds: Place and Journey in Celtic Spirituality'*, 30.
- C.S. Lewis quoted by Robert Fyall, *ibid*, 96.
- The quotation about the marginal being the centre is from Brother Ramon, SSF, *'The Heart of Prayer'*, 1995, 122-3, quoted by Martin Robinson, *ibid*, 40.
- R.L. Stevenson, *'El Dorado'* quoted by Robert Fyall, *ibid*, 1.
- In an extract from *'Sermon Eight'*, St. Columbanus, who travelled from Leinster in Ireland all over Europe wrote in 540, quoted by Ian Bradley, *ibid*, 40.
- Cintra Pemberton, *ibid*, on the place of resurrection, the significance of the Celtic mission and the quotation from Eleanor Duckett, *'The Wandering Saints'*, London, Collins, 1959, 25, 27, 30.
- John Bell *(b.1949)* and Graham Maule *(b.1958)*, *'Inspired by love and anger'*, Wild Goose Resource Group, The Iona Community.
- Daniel O'Leary quotation from *ibid*, 74.
- Gerald Hughes, *'Walk to Jerusalem'*, quoted by Martin Robinson, *ibid*,139.

bibliography

- Adam, D., *The Open Gate*, Triangle, 1994, ISBN 0-281-04767-7
- Adams, I., *Unfurling*, Canterbury Press, 2014, ISBN 978-1-84825-645-3
- Bede, *The Ecclesiastical History of the English People,* OUP, 1999, ISBN 0-19-83866-0
- Bradley, Ian, *The Celtic Way*, DLT, 1993
- Bradley, Ian, *Colonies of Heaven: Celtic Models for Today's Church*, DLT, 2000, ISBN 0-232-52337-1
- Bradley, Ian, *Pilgrimage: a Spiritual and Cultural Journey*, Lion, 2009, ISBN 978-0-7459-52703
- Brown, M., *St. Michael's Way: A Walk through Time History & Mystery,* Friends of St Michael's Way, 2016.
- Church Guides: J. Spence, *St Germans Church: A History and Guide*; *Talland Church*; N.A. Ackland & R.M. Druce, *Lanteglos by Fowey with Polruan and Bodinnick: The Story of a Parish,* Trevedda Press, 1997, ISBN 0-9521980- I-0; F.E. Burdett, *The Story of St Saviour at Polruan,* 1973, Pegagus Printers, I.D. Spreadbury; *The Church of St Fimbarrus, Fowey,* Pegasus Printers; Tywardreath PCC/ Janet Hewer, *The Parish Church of St. Andrew the Apostle, Tywardreath*; J. Rowe, *A Short History of Luxulyan Parish and the Parish Church of SS Cyriacus & Julitta; Lanivet Church: A Brief History and Guide for Visitors; St Issey Parish Church;* PCC of Padstow, *The Church of St Petroc, Padstow: A Visitor's Guide,* 2015; B. Wood, *St Merryn: Its Church and Parish;* E. Pruen, *A Guide to the Ancient Parish Church of St Eval Cornwall,* 2015; *Welcome to St Mawgan Church in the beautiful vale of Lanherne;* M. Trevenna, *A Guide to the Church of St. Mawgan-in -Pydar with Notes on the History of the Parish,* Edyvean Printers, St. Columb, 2007; M. Brown, *The Parish Church of St. Carantoc,* P & J Print, Newquay, 1996; C. Thomas, *Gwithian,* Camborne Printing and Stationary, 1964; C.P.J., *St Uny Lelant,* 1981; J.Culver, *St. Uny: Fact or Fiction,* 2003; *The John Knill Celebrations,* 2001.
- Doble, G.H, *The Saints of Cornwall, Part One: Saints of the Land End District*, Llanerfech Publishers, ISBN 1-86143-041-8
- Dowling, J., *Church Trails in Cornwall: The Padstow,* Deltor.
- Finney, J., Recovering the Past: Celtic and Roman Mission, DLT, 1996, ISBN 0-232-52083-6
- Freudenberg, J., *Visions & Vistas: Cornish saints in the Landscape,* 2012
- Fyall, R., *Travelling Hopefully*, SPCK, 1996, ISBN 0-281-04942-4
- Gildas, *The Ruin of Britain*, Philimore & Co. Ltd, 1978
- James, B., *Tales of the Saints Way,* Dyllansow Truran, 1993, ISBN 185-022-063-8.
- John, C.R., *The Saints of Cornwall,* Tabb House, 2001, ISBN 1-873951-39-6
- Lewis, H & G., *The Saints Way: Forth an Syns,* Pelican Studio, 2012, ISBN 978-0-9572340-0-0
- Low, M, *St Cuthbert's Way: A Pilgrim's Companion, Wild Goose Productions,* 1999, ISBN 1-901557-22-7
- Macfarlane, R., *The Old Ways,*

Hamish Hamilton, 2012,
- Macfarlane, R., *The Old Ways*, Hamish Hamilton, 2012, ISBN 978-0-241-14381-0
- Marsden, P., *Rising Ground*, Granta, 2014, ISBN 978-1-84708-630-3
- O'Leary, D.J., *Travelling Light: Your Journey to Wholeness*, The Columba Press, 2003, ISBN 1-85607-319-X
- Ordance Survey Cornwall Walks, Ordance survey/Jarrold Publishing, 1990, ISBN 0-319-00213-6/ISBN 0-7117-0457-0
- Ordnance Survey Explorer Maps 102, 104, 106, 107, 108
- Ordnance Survey South West Coast Path 2. North Cornwall, ISBN 978-1-84348-873-6
- Ordnance Survey South West Coast Path 3. South Cornwall, ISBN 978-1-84348-874-3
- Orme, N., *The Saints of Cornwall*, OUP, 2000, ISBN 0-19-820765-4
- Mason, J.H.N., *Walk the Cornish Coastal Path*, John Bartholomew & Son Ltd, ISBN 0-7028-0902-0
- Matthews, M; *Both Alike to Thee: The Retrival of the Mystical Way*, SPCK, 2000, ISBN 0-281-05030-9
- Mayne, M., *This Sunrise of Wonder*, Fount, 1995, ISBN 0-00-627870-1
- Miller, H., & Broadhurst, P., *The sun and the Serpent*, Pendragon Press, 1989, ISBN 0-95115183-1-3
- Mitton, M, *Restoring the Woven Cord: Strands of Christianity for the Church Today*, DLT, 1995
- Parker, Russ, *Rediscovering the Ministry of Blessing*, SPCK, 2014, ISBN 978-0-281-06981-1
- Palmer, M., *Sacred Land*, Piatkus, 2012
- Pé, Diana, *Cornwall Walks to Churches*, PP, 2004, ISBN 0-9543690-1-7
- Pemberton, Cintra, *Soulfaring: Celtic Pilgrimage Then and Now*, OSH, SPCK, 1999 ISBN 0-8192-1780-8
- Philips, A., *An Forth Keltek*, Spys A Gernow, 2009, ISBN 978-0-954851-8-6
- Plewes, J., *Gifts*, ISBN 13978-1495394409
- *Pub Walks & Cycle Rides*, AA, 2005, ISBN 978-0-7495-4449-2
- Radice, B., (ed), *The Age of Bede*, Penguin Classics, 1965, ISBN 0-14-044727 – X
- Ramm, R., *Trevose Golf and Country Club*, Trevose Ltd, 2012
- Robinson, M., *Sacred Places, Pilgrim Paths: an Anthology of Pilgrimage*, Harper Collins, 1997, ISBN 0-551-03051-8
- Sheldrake, P., *Living Between Worlds: Place and Journey in Celtic Spirituality*, DLT, 1995, ISBN 978-0-232-52119-1
- Sheldrake, P., *Spaces for the Sacred*, SCM Press, 2001, ISBN 0-334-02820-5
- *Short Walks in Cornwall*, Collins, 2011, ISBN 978-0-00-739545
- Simpson, R., *Exploring Celtic Spirituality: Historical Roots for our Future*, Hodder & Stoughton, 1995
- Smith, G., *Christian Mission in Western Society*, edited by Simon Barrow & Graeme Smith, CTBI, 2001
- St. Aubyn, J., *St Michael's Mount*, Beric Tempest & Company, St Ives, Cornwall, 1978.
- *St. Michael's Way: Forth Sen Myghal*, Cornwall County Council, 1994.
- *St. Michael's Way: Coast to Coast in West Cornwall*, Ronan Group, 2016.
- Tielhard de Chardin, *Writings Selected*, Orbis, 1999, ISBN 1-57075-248-6
- Toulson, S., *The Celtic Alternative: A Reminder of the Christianity We Lost*, Century, 1987

- Thomas, R.S., *Collected Poems 1945-1990,* Orion Books Ltd. 1993, ISBN: 0-75381-105-7
- Usher, G.B., *Places of Enchantment: Meeting God in Landscapes,* SPCK, 2012, ISBN 978-0-281-06792-3
- Walke, B., *Twenty Years at St. Hilary*, Truran, 2002, ISBN 1-85022-164-2
- Ward, B., *Pilgrimage of the Heart,* SLG press, 2001, ISBN 0-7283-0155-5
- Woods, R.J., *The Spirituality of the Celtic Saints,* Orbis, 2000, ISBN 1-57075-316-4

photography

Cover: Godrevy Lighthouse PM
Back Cover: Mexico Towans RLM

St. Germans Priory Church RH
Road to Narkus Cross PM
Pebbles, Downderry Beach PM
Nelson the Seal, Looe NM
Looe Island PM
Talland Church PM
Lansallos RM
Cove at Lansallos RH
Lansallos Churchyard cross RH
Lantic Bay PM
St. Saviour's Chapel, Polruan RH
Polruan-Fowey Ferry PM
Fowey from Polruan PM
Readymoney Cove PM
The Saints Way signs RH
Eden, rainforest biome PM
Eden, rainforest biome 2 PM
Eden biomes PM
Treffry viaduct PM
Boulders near Luxulyan RH
Give Way sign PM
St. Ingunger Cross PM
Fenton Pitts Cross PM
VT Lani Way marker PM
Tregustick Ford PM
St. Breock Wind Farm PM
Longstone, St. Breock Downs PM
St. Issey Church PM
Blable sign PM
Font at St. Merryn Church PM
Padstow harbour PM
Trevone PM
Constantine Well PM
Constantine Chapel RH
St. Eval Church PM
Porthcothan LI
St. Eval Church PM
Shell cross, St. Eval Church PM
Aeroplane KN
Coast path from Trevarrian PM
Watergate Bay PM
Porth Beach PM
Towan Beach RLM
Holiday bears PM
River Gannel - George Hiles
Penpol Tidal Footbridge PM
Holywell Bay RH
The Holy Well RH
Cubert Church RH
St. Piran's Oratory PM
St. Piran's Celtic cross RH
Helicopter RH
Wheal Coates PM
Coast path RH
Porthtreath harbour RH
North Cliffs PM
North Cliffs RH
Godrevy Lighthouse PM
Lobster pot NM
Hayle estuary MH
Hayle sands RH
Trencrom PM
Carbis Bay MH
St. Michael's way signs PM
The Bowl Rock PM
Approaching the Red River Ford PM
Eden valley PM
Marazion Marshes PM
St. Michael's Mount PM
The causeway PM
St. Michael's Mount RH
St. Piran's Oratory Cross PM

RH: Roger Hamlin
PM: Penny Marns
NM: Nigel Marns
LI: Lisa Isted
KN: Kirsten Norfolk
MH: Martin Holland
RLM: Rosanna Marns
RM: Robert Marns